D1279348

The Pursuit of Race
and Gender Equity in
American Academe

The Pursuit of Race and Gender Equity in American Academe

Stephanie L. Witt

DISCARD

PRAEGER

New York
Westport, Connecticut
London

Library of Congress Cataloging-in-Publication Data

Witt, Stephanie L.
   The pursuit of race and gender equity in American academe / by
Stephanie L. Witt.
      p.   cm.
   Includes bibliographical references.
   ISBN 0-275-93553-1
   1. Universities and colleges—United States—Faculty.   2. Afro-
American college teachers—United States.   3. Women college
teachers—United States.   4. Affirmative action programs—United
States.   I. Title.
   LB2331.72.W57   1990
   378.1'2'0973—dc20   90-7014

British Library Cataloguing in Publication Data is available.

Library of Congress Catalog Card Number: 90-7014
ISBN: 0-275-93553-1

First published in 1990

Praeger Publishers, One Madison Avenue, New York, NY 10010
An imprint of Greenwood Publishing Group, Inc.

Printed in the United States of America

The paper used in this book complies with the
Permanent Paper Standard issued by the National
Information Standards Organization (Z39.48-1984).

10 9 8 7 6 5 4 3 2 1

For Leslie

Contents

Acknowledgments

Many thanks are due to the members of the Interdisciplinary Research Unit on Faculty Stress and Productivity at Washington State University, as well as the Office of Grants and Research Development at that institution for making this research possible. Nicholas Lovrich, Earl Smith, Walt Gmelch, Mary Welsh Jordan, and Phyllis Kay Wilke all participated in the gathering of the National Faculty Stress Studies. Without their hard work this project would not have been possible.

I am also indebted to Nicholas Lovrich, Mary Ann E. Steger, and Terry Cook for their review of earlier versions of this manuscript. Their time and critiques of this work are appreciated. Any errors or faults that remain, however, are my own.

I would also like to acknowledge the support and assistance provided by the Boise State University computing center for their help in the preparation of this manuscript.

Finally, I should recognize the support and encouragement given to me by my friends who have listened patiently to my frustrations about this project, and yet always believed that I would finish. Thanks.

The Pursuit of Race
and Gender Equity in
American Academe

1

Introduction

The purpose of this chapter is threefold. The first purpose is to provide the reader with a general overview of the policy of affirmative action. The official statements and policy clarifications supplied by the U.S. Commission on Civil Rights are relied upon to explicate the rationale and official "purposes of state" underlying this public policy. The second purpose of the introduction is to provide the reader with a general conception of the historical progress (or lack thereof) made in increasing the numbers of women and minority faculty in American universities in recent decades. Several studies outlining this employment situation will be discussed briefly, so that the policy of affirmative action can be understood relative to its "success" or "failure" within academe. The third purpose of this introduction is to set forth the general outline of the study. A short description of each of the chapters to follow is given, permitting the reader to command a full picture of the purposes and methods of study employed throughout as she or he considers each chapter in moving through the entire work.

AFFIRMATIVE ACTION

While some would mark the 1948 Dixiecrat revolt as the beginning of civil rights for blacks as an active political issue in U.S. politics, most contemporary writing in this area reflects the view that the United States has been committed to an active public policy of pursuing the goal of greater racial equality in our society since the 1960s. The passage of the Civil Rights Act of 1964 is broadly viewed as a major step in the direction of finally securing for blacks and other minorities the legal protections putatively guaranteed them in the Constitution and post-Civil War legislation. Since enactment of this statutory declaration of a right to equal opportunity in American society, the Congress, the courts and the presidency have taken appropriate governmental steps to strike down many of the remaining obstacles to equal opportunity that continued to confront minorities in this country in the 1960s. One important--and quite controversial--aspect of this effort to enhance equality of opportunity for those who were historically victims of unjust discrimination was the development of the policy of affirmative action.

According to the United States Commission on Civil Rights, affirmative action refers to "any measure, beyond simple termination of a discriminatory practice, adopted to correct or compensate for past or present discrimination or to prevent discrimination from recurring in the future" (U.S. Civil Rights Commission 1979:179). The logic used by the Civil Rights Commission hinges on the recognition that to simply remove discriminatory barriers is not enough to ensure that equity will be achieved in the work force. Many writers, discussing the challenges that affirmative action seeks to meet, cite the familiar story of the two runners in a race, one of whom is shackled at the ankles. Halfway through the race the judge notices that one of the runners is shackled and undoes the chains. The story then posits the questions faced in examining affirmative action: Should the judge give the shackled runner a 'head start' in the race to make up for the damage of having been shackled? Should both runners start together with no special help? What, ultimately, would make the race "fair"? The Civil Rights Commission maintains that affirmative action recognizes that to make the race "fair" some help has to be given to the previously shackled runner to make up for past disadvantages. Members of the Commission write:

> The justification for affirmative action to secure equal access to the job market lies in the need to overcome the effects of past discrimination by the employers, unions, colleges and universities who are asked to undertake such action. It rests also in the practical need to assure that young people whose lives have been marred by discrimination in public education and other institutions are not forever barred from the opportunity to realize their potential and to become useful

and productive citizens (U.S. Civil Rights Commission 1979:189).

Using this fundamental logic, affirmative action policies have been developed in the areas of student admissions to universities and professional schools and employment practices for both private and public employers, which are intended to offset disadvantages historically suffered by women and minorities through past discrimination. As the next section of this introduction will indicate, however, despite the intended outcomes of such policies, the overall impact of affirmative action programs in higher education has been relatively modest in terms of increasing the numbers of minority scholars and professors in American universities and professional schools.

MINORITIES AND WOMEN IN HIGHER EDUCATION

This study will focus on affirmative action policies developed in institutions of higher education that affect faculty conditions of employment. The study entails a close examination of the attitudes of university faculty about this public policy issue. Although formal affirmative action plans and a mixture of voluntary, compulsory and court-moderated preferential employment policies have been in place in American universities since the early 1970s, actual progress toward the achievement of equitable numbers of women and minorities among university faculty has been painfully slow. Shirley Vining Brown reports in her study of minority university faculty that the number of black faculty in American universities has actually been *declining* in recent years. She notes that "black full-time faculty positions decreased from 19,674 to 18,827 between 1977-83, and the decline is apparent in both public (-6.2 percent) and private (-11.3 percent) four-year institutions (Brown 1988:1).

Joseph Hankin reports statistical evidence from an Equal Employment Opportunity Commission study in which it was found that minorities comprised only 9.25 percent of university faculties nationwide (Hankin 1985:4). Examining minority progress by academic discipline yields even more dismal results. Rodney Reed reports that in the fields of science and engineering, tenured minority faculty are distributed such that blacks comprise only 1 percent of the faculty. The number of black faculty is equally small (1 percent), according to Reed, in the humanities (Reed 1985:27). The situation in the sciences, engineering, the humanities, and even the social sciences and education--two areas where minorities are most in evidence--is compounded by the fact that the total absolute number of minority faculty is actually declining rather than rising (Nagel 1988).

Many scholars point to the "supply problem" when discussing the shortage of minority faculty in American universities. In their work, *American Professors: A National Resource Imperiled*, Howard Bowen and Jack Schuster provide a comprehensive look at America's university faculty. Bowen and Schuster address the issue of the numbers and proportions of minority faculty in American universities using national statistics and field interviews from across the nation. They note that there had been a slow upward trend in the proportion of minority faculty, rising from 6.2 percent of the faculty in 1973 to 9.1 percent in 1980 (Bowen and Schuster 1986:59). They also note, however, that the future outlook does not look bright. Bowen and Schuster, along with many of the black university faculty they interview, highlight the fact that the declining proportions of black undergraduates and graduate students in American institutions of higher education, and the declining interest in academic careers among those few black students who are in school constitute the chief problems in attaining future increases in minority faculty (Bowen and Schuster 1986:153).

The number of black students "in the pipeline" appears to be falling, as fewer minority students pursue graduate studies or plan careers in academia if they are currently enrolled as graduate students. Brown reports that there has been "a substantial decline in the black doctorate pool during the 1980's" (Brown 1988:1). The *New York Times* cites the findings of the American Council on Education which reports that black enrollment in higher education institutions peaked in 1980 at 1.1 million students (out of a total of 11.8 million students). The *Times* goes on to say that by 1986 there were 12.5 million students in total, but that the number of black students had fallen by 30,000 from the high of 1.1 million in 1980 (Daniels 1989:1). The goal of increasing the number of minority faculty in academia will certainly grow more challenging as the numbers of available minority scholars upon which to draw grows ever smaller. It is also unlikely that funding for minority scholars will increase in the near future given the cutbacks made necessary by the budget deficit. As H. George Frederickson notes in his *New Public Administration*:

> The problem of productivity, coupled with the problem of revenue and expenditure cutbacks, could lessen the potentials for social equity. If there is less and less generally, there will be less and less to go around. If history is any guide, under conditions of cutback or austerity, those

at the lower end of the social and economic spectrum receive the least (Frederickson 1980:120).

The situation for women faculty (both black and white) is somewhat more promising in total numbers. Bowen and Schuster report that women comprised 30 percent of the faculty in American universities (Bowen and Schuster 1986:57). Other researchers note, however, that women tend to be concentrated in smaller institutions and satellite campuses, which removes them from the major research institutions at which academic recognition is often gained (Fox 1984:247). In addition, Fox notes that women are concentrated in the lower academic ranks, comprising 52.8 percent of the instructors, 35.3 percent of the assistant professors, 20.6 percent of the associate professors and only 10.6 percent of the full professors nationwide (1984:248). As noted in regard to minority faculty above, increasing a prolonged period of fiscal austerity in higher education budgets will likely delay the pursuit of equitable numbers of women faculty across all ranks in U.S. universities.

OVERVIEW OF THE STUDY

This study will examine the attitudes of a national sample of university faculty about the policy of affirmative action as it is implemented in their respective college or university. University faculty have been chosen as the subject of this study because of their relatively unique ability to make collegial hiring and promotional decisions, and their operation within a system widely presumed to be based on merit (as indicated by scientific contribution, scholarly publications, attraction of funding for research, teaching excellence, etc.). The university represents a synthesis of a high social purpose, a system based on meritocratic achievement and a forum for the legitimate pursuit of individualistic self-interest in the pursuit of one's academic career. As such, university faculty are a particularly appropriate subpopulation from which to learn more about the workings of more general social dynamics. The confrontation of meritocracy and the practice of compensatory consideration poses for the individuals involved in the hiring, tenure and promotional processes of the academy some often weighty conflicts between competing valid claims of individuals and the broader social order. These attitudes about affirmative action in academia will be examined within a framework that outlines the larger issues involved in the policy of affirmative action to promote equality of opportunity for the historical victims of discrimination. This analysis will be accomplished by outlining the competing values in American society which the policy of affirmative action serves to bring into conflict for individuals and for society. Chapter 2 will examine this conflict of values as it manifests itself in a contemporary liberal society. The chief competing values of concern are the primacy of the individual, on the one hand, and the need for collective advancement of social equity or fairness on the other. Affirmative action faces the difficult multiple challenges of: (1) enhancing the protection of minority individual rights; (2) avoiding "trampling" on the equal protection rights of white males; (3) ensuring that the final distribution of employment opportunity is such as to encourage both the highly qualified nonprotected and the upwardly striving disadvantaged group person to view the security system of employment opportunity as fair to them; and (4) ensuring the accomplishment of societal tasks for which schools, colleges, universities, agencies, corporations and the professions are responsible in as efficient a manner as possible. It is the conflict of these important competing values that makes affirmative action rather problematic in liberal societies.

The third chapter of this study will examine the resolution of some of these societal conflicts which have been framed as issues in statutory construction and constitutional law. The Supreme Court has addressed the issue of affirmative action directly in several major cases, including some that involve higher education specifically. Its decisions in these cases in large part reflect an attempt to achieve a workable balance between these competing values discussed above. Chapter 3 will outline briefly the major cases involving affirmative action, and discuss some of the scholarly commentary which speculates on the likely long-term consequences of these several decisions on the future operation of American colleges, universities and professional schools.

The fourth chapter will describe the empirical data analyzed in this study. This research was made possible by a grant from the W.W. Kellogg Foundation[1] and the Office of Grants and Research Development (Graduate School) at Washington State University. This study is based on the 1986 National Faculty Stress Study and a supplemental survey of black academics conducted by the fellows of the Interdisciplinary Research Unit on Faculty Stress and Productivity based at Washington State University.[2] The 1986 study contains many questions relating to affirmative action in the university and the perception of professional and career advantages and disadvantages faced by minority and women faculty. The methodology used in this analysis was developed out of a great labor- and time-intensive search for "matched pairs" of faculty taken from the larger collection of respondents and the supplemental minority scholar survey. Respondents to the 1986 study were hand-matched on the basis of race, gender, tenure status, type of institution, academic discipline, age and marital status to yield a final sample of 246 pairs of faculty matched on the above dimensions. A description of the survey items and their construction, and an explanation of how those items are operationalized into analytical variables and placed into the larger framework discussed above are also contained in this section of the study.

Chapters 5 and 6 explain the data analysis and the results obtained from the examination of university faculty attitudes about affirmative action and minority and women scholars. The results indicate that the objective self-interest of university faculty members as beneficiaries (women and minorities) or as the bearers of costs (white males) is related to the general evaluation of affirmative action policy in both its impact on American universities in general and on an individual's career. Significant differences in the perception of university faculty with regard to affirmative action exist between racial and gender categorical groups. This finding contradicts the supposed existence of a race- and gender-neutral academy. To the contrary, membership in a categorical group makes a great difference in the evaluation of affirmative action policies.

NOTES

1. A pilot study for the research reported here was conducted on a nationwide sample of faculty under the auspices of a grant from the W.W. Kellogg Foundation to support research into faculty service activities and related stress outcomes being conducted by Washington Statue University Professors Walt Gmelch (College of Education) and Nicholas Lovrich (Department of Political Science). Both Gmelch and Lovrich were employed as faculty fellows under the Kellogg grant provisions.

2. Three consecutive annual Interdisciplinary Research Unit Grants-in-Aid were made to Walt Gmelch, Nicholas Lovrich and Earl Smith (Department of Comparative American Cultures) by the Office of Grants and Research Development (Graduate School) at Washington State University. Several publications have resulted from this research, including the following: Walter Gmelch, Nicholas P. Lovrich and P. Kaye Wilke, "Stress in Academe: A National Perspective," *Research in Higher Education* (1984); Phyllis Kay Wilke, Walter Gmelch and Nicholas Lovrich, "Stress

and Productivity: Evidence of the Inverted U Function in a National Study of University Faculty," *Public Productivity Review* (1985); Walter Gmelch, Phyllis Kay Wilke and Nicholas P. Lovrich, "Dimensions of Stress Among University Faculty: Factor Analytic Results from a National Study," *Research in Higher Education* (1986); Stephanie L. Witt and Nicholas P. Lovrich, "Sources of Stress Among Faculty: Gender Differences," The *Review of Higher Education* (1988); and Earl Smith and Stephanie L. Witt, "Faculty Attitudes Toward Affirmative Action: The Academic Ethos in Question," *The Western Journal of Black Studies* (forthcoming).

2

Liberal Societies and Affirmative Action

The policy known as "affirmative action" serves as an excellent focus for the examination of competing--and often incompatible-- values in contemporary societies. How shall a just society of high (postindustrial) economic status maintain its commitment to both the sanctity of the individual and the achievement of an equitable final distribution of well-being across gender and ethnic groups? Affirmative action is intended to promote societal equity by ending the continued "underutilization" of historically disadvantaged groups--in particular, women and racial minorities. The achievement of this more equitable final distribution of employment opportunities for the former victims of discrimination, however, can come at the expense of certain important procedural "equal protection" rights for white males. Herein lies the conflict of competing values created by the policy of affirmative action: how to most appropriately balance the rights of equitable treatment of individuals against the desire to achieve a final distribution of well-being across historically advantaged and disadvantaged groups that is more equitable than in the past. While a number of countries are seeking to deal with such issues, the United States has the longest experience of this sort of compensatory employment public policy (Heidenheimer et al. 1975:130-57).

Citizens of the United States have come to value highly the fact that their individual rights to equitable treatment are secured by well-established and legally enforceable procedural safeguards. Within this general framework, individuals are seen as being free to pursue their own personal interests in a context of fair or equal competition affording opportunity for just rewards for effort and/or merit. Such procedural safeguards for equal opportunity are widely believed, in fact, to provide the most effective means for individuals to secure their own interests and promote the general welfare of society writ large. The pursuit of self-interest in conditions of equal competition, then, constitutes a fundamental feature of both the procedural safeguards accorded individuals in American society and the belief in the fairness of the outcomes of such competition. As a result of this legitimate exercise of the self-interest dynamic, affirmative action policies can beget a conflict not only of a society-wide distributional nature, as noted by Arthur Okun in his classic *Equality and Efficiency: The Big Tradeoff* (1975), but also conflict on an individual "micro-level." By this I mean that individuals--particularly white males--may face a conflict within themselves stemming from the incompatibility of their perceived self-interest (usually securing an admission to a college, professional school, job or career advancement) and the more collective societal equity interests served by a compensatory justice-oriented public policy such as affirmative action (Lasch 1979:55-64).

This chapter will discuss affirmative action policies in terms of these two levels of conflicting values. First, the societal-level dilemma of securing procedual fairness for individuals while also achieving acceptable final distributions across historically advantaged and disadvantaged groups in a liberal society will be discussed. Theories of just distributions of social goods that attempt to achieve this balance of individual rights versus collective needs--particularly those of John Rawls's *A Theory of Justice* and Michael Sandel's *Liberalism and the Limits of Justice*--will be outlined briefly for their insights into this macro level conflict in liberal societies.

Second, the micro level conflict, that of the self-interest of individuals versus the social equity needs of the collective, will be described. By determining the sources of an individual's attitudes about affirmative action--that is, whether those attitudes derive from and reflect self-interest or rather mirror a concern for achieving equity in the collective--any individual-level conflict (or cross-pressures) can be drawn out. The current debate in the social sciences about how best to understand motivations underlying political attitudes and behavior will be investigated in the context of affirmative action. Approaches such as "public choice," which place self-interest as primary, versus approaches premised on the belief that individuals act out of genuine concern for the welfare of the collective (such as those developed in the work of Steven Kelman) will be outlined to gain some insight into this individual-level conflict. The requirements of civic virtue as opposed to the legitimate pursuit of self-interest--a question that separated parties to the constitutional convention two centuries ago (Rohr 1987)--will be revisited in this analysis of contemporary affirmative action policies.

LIBERAL SOCIETIES AND AFFIRMATIVE ACTION: MACRO-LEVEL ISSUES

In many ways, a prime challenge for modern liberalism involves balancing the primacy of the individual so central to liberal thought with the needs of a modern, complex world. The difficulty in achieving this balance stems from the economic and social inequalities that result from marketplace-dictated distributions in a liberal, free enterprise society. As Thomas Nagel (1977:8) points out:

> Liberalism has therefore come under increasing attack in recent years, on the ground that the familiar principles of equal treatment, with its meritocratic conception of relevant differences, seems too weak to combat the inequalities dispensed by nature and the ordinary workings of the social system.

Affirmative action is relevant to Nagel's discussion precisely because it cuts across those important liberal values of inalienable individual rights, meritocracy and social equity. It is in discussions of how to justify the policy of affirmative action--and related concepts such as merit, equality and desert--that the conflict involving the preservation of individual rights while still acheiving acceptable final distributions of social goods becomes clear.

Many of the writers who address this conflict do so from a framework of economic and social justice. Arthur and Shaw write, for example, that "justice, then, is an important subclass of morality in general, a subclass which generally involves appeals to the overlapping notions of rights, fairness, equality, or desert" (Arthur and Shaw 1987:4).

One of the most important scholars of economic justice within the liberal tradition is John Rawls. His *A Theory of Justice* (1971) is a benchmark from which many other writers begin their investigations of questions of justice in liberal societies. The "original position," a hypothesized state from which people can act from a position of fairness (through a veil of ignorance), and the "difference principle" in which unequal distributions of societal benefits are supposed to either benefit all or help the least advantaged, are both ways of trying to make the final distribution of goods in society more equitable while not ceding the importance of individual rights. As Rawls notes, "the idea [of the two principles of justice] is to redress the bias of contingencies in the direction of equality" (Rawls 1978:38).

Rawls's theory, like those of all other liberal theorists, retains the primacy of the individual. Michael Sandel correctly notes that both Rawls and Dworkin, another very prominent contemporary philosopher, retain as a fundamental aspect of their work this traditional position of liberal thought: "Dworkin, like Rawls, believes that no social policy can be justified, however well it serves the general welfare, if it violates individual rights" (Sandel 1982:135). In further keeping with the liberal tradition, Rawls assumes the legitimacy of the self-interested behavior of individuals, and constructs his theory to fit the hypothesized proclivity for rational action on the part of humans. He writes:

> They [principles of justice] are the principles that free and rational persons concerned to further their own interests would accept in an initial position of equality as defining the fundamental terms of their association (Rawls 1978:18).

Modern liberal scholars typically start from a position of opposition to the tenets of utilitarianism, according to which the rights of individuals can be subordinated to the needs of society if that would increase the total amount of benefits relative to total costs. Sandel writes:

> Rawls's and Dworkin's positions are similar in a more general way as well. Both are rights-based theories, defined in explicit opposition to utilitarian conceptions, and seek to defend certain individual claims against the calculus of social interests (Sandel 1988:138).

It is in dealing with this "calculus of social interests" that affirmative action becomes so problematic for liberals. Affirmative action would seem to take the rights of some individuals (white males) and subordinate those rights of equal protection in open competition serving to reward merit to a larger social need of increasing equitable distribution of work force opportunities. As Cohen et al. note, "the most important argument against preferential treatment is that it subordinates the individual's right to equal treatment to broader social aims" (1988:viii). The justification for most governmental actions in a liberal state must be compatible with the primary need to protect individual rights against most claims of the collective. As Cohen et al. further note, "there may be a way to defend group compensation and liability without appealing to individual justifications, but it would appear to depend on illegitimate personification of collectivities" (Cohen et al. 1988:ix).

Michael Sandel critiques the liberal theory of justice as developed by Rawls for failing to deal adequately with the ultimate conflict between the rights of the individual as developed by liberal theory, and the demands of the larger society. He writes:

> As bearers of rights, where rights are trumps, we think of ourselves as freely choosing, individual selves, unbound by obligations antecedent to rights, or the agreements we make. And yet, as citizens of the procedural republic that secures these rights, we find ourselves implicated willy-nilly in a formidable array of dependencies and expectations we did not choose and increasingly reject (Sandel 1988:94).

Sandel criticizes the difference principle of Rawls's theory because it violates the primacy of the individual so important to liberal theories. Rawls assumes that assets that individuals have are only "accidentally" theirs from a moral point of view. That is to say, individuals do not "deserve" to be born rich or white, for example; it is a morally arbitrary circumstance that they were. Rawls writes:

> We see then that the difference principle represents, in effect, an agreement to regard the distribution of natural talents as a common asset and to share in the benefits of this distribution, whatever it turns out to be (Rawls 1978:39).

Sandel's problem with Rawls stems from the fact that Rawls claims that since one's assets are only an accident of birth, the society can therefore make claims on the exercise of those assets. He states: Simply because I, as an individual, do not have a privileged claim on the assets accidentally residing 'here' it does not follow that everyone in the world collectively does" (Sandel 1988:89).

Sandel applies this criticism to Dworkin's discussion of affirmative action by noting that Dworkin must be able to describe who the relevant "subject of possession" is for the assets accidentally residing in any one individual (1988:144). He concludes that since there is no adequate justification for the society's making claims on the assets arbitrarily possessed by individuals, that liberalism in the end resembles utilitarianism--using some as means for others' ends--and thereby violating one of liberalism's basic principles (Sandel 1988:144).

In summary, liberalism in its modern variants has difficulty justifying a policy such as affirmative action, which requires the subordination of some fundamental individual rights and interests for the achievement of some important societal goal. Scholars of liberalism seek to rectify inequities in the final distribution of social goods with devices such as the "original position" and the "difference principle," but in the end may face continuing difficulties in maintaining the unviolated importance of the individual and the perceived self-interest of an individual relative to the needs of society. The same problematic meshing of individual and societal interests that bedevils contemporary liberal thinkers likely possesses an analog in the individual consciences of liberal white males--the inheritors of advantaged social positions in an individualistic, competitive society that has too long tolerated institutionalized racism and gender inequality. To this topic we now turn our attention.

THE LIBERAL TRADITION, SELF-INTEREST AND AFFIRMATIVE ACTION: MICRO LEVEL ISSUES

Moving now to the micro-level, this section will establish the importance of the conflict of self-interest versus the needs of the collective within individuals in contemporary liberal societies. The institutions of U.S. government, and the understanding of politics that Americans tend to hold, cannot be understood without reference to the liberal political tradition. This tradition emphasizes the importance of the individual relative to the state. As Max Skidmore notes, "the essence of liberalism is its concentration on the individual" (Skidmore 1978:11). While Plato and Aristotle clearly considered the interests of the state and the citizen to be one and the same, the liberal tradition made a major departure from this conception of the polis in focusing instead on those interests, claims and powers that individuals have against the government and its interest (Skidmore 1978:13).

In this approach, in which the individual is prior to and capable of withdrawing consent from the state, the importance of individuals acting in their own self-interest becomes paramount. Bellah et al., in describing the essential features of the contemporary civil religion of Americans, point out the importance of self-interested behavior to the theory of the social contract as developed by John Locke. The philosophical writings of Locke deeply influenced the founders of the U.S. constitution, whose essential message was summarized by Bellah and his colleagues in the words: "The individual is prior to society, which comes into existence only through the voluntary contract of individuals trying to maximize their own self-interest" (Bellah et al. 1985:143).

Social contract theory posits a way for the state to be created such that each individual's consent is implied and their self-interest is served. The importance of the individual in Locke's theory was, of course, a belief shared by most of the founders of the U.S. political system (Horwitz 1979). The primacy of the belief in the legitimacy and pervasiveness of self-interested individual pursuits in the political sphere is reflected in the formation of the U.S. government. The Declaration of Independence, for example, emphasized the importance of the individual as the basic unit of the polity (Skidmore 1978:46). The tendency for humans to act in their own self-interest was of course, both acknowledged and feared by the founders of the U.S. republic. James Madison wrote:

> Ambition must be made to counteract ambition. The interest of the man must be connected with the constitutional rights of the place. In may be a reflection on human nature, that such devices should be necessary to control the abuses of government. But what is government itself but the greatest of all reflections on human nature? If men were angels, no government would be necessary (Madison: *Federalist #51*).

As if reiterating the fears of Madison about the pursuit of self interest, Bellah et al. contend that American culture, as it has evolved over time, has developed an increasing focus on the pursuit of self-interest to the exclusion of the consideration of collective needs.

They point to the fundamental difficulty that Americans have in discussing issues of the common good. They contend that American culture defines "personality, achievement, and the purpose of human life in ways that leave the individual suspended in glorious but terrifying isolation" (Bellah et al. 1985:6). This isolation stems from the pursuit of individual interests to the near exclusion of common or group interests. Since each individual will develop and follow his or her own self-interest, collective decision-making under circumstances wherein individual interests conflict becomes difficult. As Bellah et al. point out, "In a world of potentially conflicting self-interests, no one can really say that one value system is better than another" (Bellah et al. 1985:7). This leaves the American culture, in the opinion of Bellah et al., incapable of discussing these issues of the common good. They contend that in politics, as well as sometimes in interpersonal relationships, "the person who thinks in terms of the common good is a 'sucker' in a situation where each individual is trying to pursue his or her own interests" (Bellah et al. 1985:8).

This is a common characterization of liberal societies, in which no one conception of the 'good' is allowed to predominate (see Barber 1979). As Jeffrey Stout points out, "Communitarians and Liberals alike tend to view liberal society as centered in the idea that we can get along without what Cicero called 'an agreement with respect to justice and a partnership for a common good'" (Stout 1986:49). Liberal societies and liberal scholars reject a *telos* (ultimate end) for society. As Sheldon Wolin (1960) contends, the 'architectonic' nature of politics and society is gone. Agreement, instead, is based on procedural requirements instead of substantive requirements for an 'end state.' Bellah et al. highlight this tendency to focus on procedural issues in their interviews with a cross-section of Americans. They note of Wayne Bauer, one of the interview subjects upon which their report is based, that he is unable to describe what "justice" is in American society beyond the purely procedural terms of giving everyone a fair chance (Bellah et al. 1985:19).

Contemporary Americans, according to Bellah et al., lack a language to understand or discuss substantive justice. This inability to discuss substantive issues of just distributions is very much in line with liberal societies' rejection of a particular version of the 'good' or final distribution of goods. In their discussion of justice as an important value to Americans, Bellah et al. (1985:25) summarize this reliance on procedural justice over substantive justice:

> Our American traditions encourage us to think of justice as a matter of equal opportunites for every individual to pursue whatever he or she understands by happiness. Equal opportunities are guaranteed by fair laws and political procedures--laws and procedures applied in the same way to everyone. But this way of thinking about justice does not in itself contain a vision of what the distribution of goods in a society would end up looking like if individuals had an equal chance to pursue their interests.

Affirmative action, then, is problematic for individual Americans to understand because it displaces the straightforward emphasis on equal procedural guarantees with a preferential decision process intended to create change so as to make more equitable the final distribution of goods in society.

The idea that Americans tend to think overwhelmingly in terms of self-interested, nonsubstantive dimensions of important issues in their public lives is viewed as highly regrettable by Bellah et al. Whether this proclivity toward self-interested motivations is viewed with despair or delight, however, this tendency toward rational conduct is taken for granted by a growing number of practicing social scientists in their studies and explanations of human behavior. The growing dominance of the self-interest approach to the understanding of human behavior in academia is well described by Steven Kelman. He outlines how assumptions of microeconomic theory have been extended to an analysis of the political process (Kelman 1987:81). The primary assumption from microeconomic theory is, of course, that "people's choices are motivated by self-interested maximization" (Kelman 1987:81). Kelman traces the growth of the "public choice" approach, the name for social science approaches using microeconomic assumptions. His account begins with Anthony Downs's application of economic assumptions to actors in the political system in *An Economic Theory of Democracy* (1957), then continues with Buchanan and Tullock's classic *The Calculus of Consent* (1962). Kelman then describes two other more recent important works embodying the public choice approach: *Congress: the Electoral Connection* (1974) by David Mayhew and *Congress: Keystone of the Washington Establishment* (1977) by Morris Fiorina. Kelman notes, somewhat sardonically, that in the course of this progression the advocates of public choice have become "less humble" in their explications of their approach (Kelman 1987:84-85). Public choice, with its focus on the pursuit of self-interest, has become a major approach in the social sciences.

Public choice is not, however, the dominant paradigm or approach to the study of social behavior and attitudes prevalent in the social sciences today. The idea that humans act out of concern for some collective, whether the polis or the church or the state, is as historically rooted as the assumption of self-interest. Certainly, ancient Greek conceptions of citizenship contained the assumption that citizens often act out of concern for the polis as a collective, subordinating their self-interest for the pursuit of the polis's advancement or betterment when required by necessity. Recently, a number of scholars have taken note of the inappropriateness of overreliance on the public choice approach. As Gary Orren (1988:24) points out: "the single most compelling and counterintuitive discovery of research on political attitudes and behavior over the last thirty years is how weak an influence self-interest actually exerts. Evidence has steadily accumulated that ideas and values are autonomous and do not merely rationalize action in accordance with self-interest." Steven Kelman outlines some of the research findings alluded to by Orren. He notes that in research conducted by Kinder and Kieweit (1979), individual attitudes about national economic conditions are not tied to the individual's personal economic condition (and, presumably, self-interest), but rather are correlated with the individual's perception of the "economic condition of society as a whole" (Kelman 1987:89). Other research findings reaching similar conclusions--such as studies of attitudes regarding National Health Insurance and Kelman's own examination of the motivations for entering the public service--lend additional support to the idea that self-interest is *not* the primary motivator for much human behavior related to issues affecting the interest of the polity (Kelman 1987:90).

Bellah et al. point out that the American cultural tradition contains, in addition to the importance of self-interest and the individual, a respect for and desire to achieve a sense of community. This sense of community, however, sometimes conflicts with the very strong sense of the autonomy of the individual that American culture values. Bellah et al. (1985:256) write:

> American culture has long been marked by acute ambivalence about the meshing of self-reliance and community; and the nation's history shows a similar ambivalence over the question of how to combine individual autonomy and the interrelationships of a complex modern economy.

Turning again to affirmative action as a public policy--the conflict on an individual level (for white males especially) becomes one of balancing one's own self-interest with the needs and demands of the community as expressed in contemporary law. This balancing of demands is made problematic by our culture's emphasis on individual autonomy, the pursuit of self-interest and the celebration of procedural justice to the near exclusion of substantive justice issues. However, postindustrial society requires both a high degree of interdependence among citizens and a high degree of concern for postindustrial values--including that of racial equity (Inglehart and Rabier 1986). How do citizens think and react when these private sacrifices for collective betterment and social justice are required of them? This study will ask this fundamental question: Is affirmative action a policy that individuals conceptualize and form opinions about based on their perceived self-interest, or do they conceptualize this policy in terms of what they believe will most fully benefit the community as a whole?

The next section of this study will review other scholarship on the attitudes Americans hold about affirmative action in particular, and related issues of equality among the races and across genders in general. It will be shown that the deeply seated conflicts among important American values discussed above are in many ways reflected in the attitudes expressed by Americans in various circumstances entailing matters of distributional justice. An exploration of the extent to which these conflicts are reflected in the attitudes of a national sample of university faculty regarding affirmative action will follow this next overview.

ATTITUDES TOWARD ISSUES OF EQUALITY AND AFFIRMATIVE ACTION

Paul Sniderman and Michael Gray Hagen, in their book *Race and Inequality*, chart the changes in the attitudes of Americans with regard to several issues related to race relations. They note that in 1964 one in every four Americans was opposed to open housing, but that by 1976 85 percent of the U.S. adult public believed that blacks had the right to live wherever they could afford to buy property (Sniderman and Hagen 1985:5). They also chart the changes in attitudes regarding the integration of schools, noting that whereas less than one-half of white Americans supported integrated schools in the 1950s this number had increased to two-thirds by the end of the 1960s (Sniderman and Hagen 1987:5). Finally, they mark the enormous change in attitudes about equal opportunity in employment. In the mid-1940s fewer than one-half of white Americans supported equal opportunity in employment, but by the early 1970s 95 percent of white Americans supported this idea (Sniderman and Hagen 1987:6). It would seem, then, that in the abstract Americans have become markedly more supportive of racial equality over time. Discovering what limits there might be to this increased support for societal racial equity, however, is yet another question.

When Americans are polled about the specific policy of affirmative action, some limits to their support of greater racial equality become apparent. As Lipset and Schneider pointed out in their 1978 review of previous studies of the public's attitudes about affirmative action:

there can be no doubt that a large number of White Americans have come to accept the proposition that discrimination in hiring is wrong and that govenment should guarantee operation of the competitive merit or achievement principle by outlawing such discrimination. But every major national study shows that a sizeable majority of Americans are also opposed to remedying the effects of past discrimination by giving any special consideration in hiring or school admissions (Lipset and Schneider 1978:40).

Gallup reports that Americans consistently oppose affirmative action when responding to questions about substituting "preferential treatment" for hiring by "ability." In 1984, for example, 84 percent of the respondents indicated that hiring and admissions should be done on the basis of ability alone, while only ten percent thought that preferential treatment should be used (Gallup 1984:29). In reference to a particular Supreme Court ruling Gallup reported that Americans disagreed with a court decision upholding affirmative action by a ratio of two to one. Although whites opposed the finding (63 percent disapproving, 29 percent approving), the majority of both blacks and other non-whites supported the decision, with 56 percent and 57 percent respectively approving of the court's action (Gallup 1987:19). It is possible, of course, that the wording of Gallup's question may have biased the response in a negative direction by using the words "preferential treatment." Similar findings, however, are reported in a 1983 study of college students in which 66 percent of blacks and only 31 percent of whites felt that providing preferences to minorities was a good idea (Selzer and Thompson 1985:8).

In their study of attitudes about affirmative action in the Washington, D.C. area, Seltzer and Thompson asked respondents a variety of questions about issues related to both racial equality in general and affirmative action programs specifically. They report that a substantial majority of both whites and blacks believe that the government ought to "see to it that people who have been discriminated against in the past get a better break in the future," with 70.3 percent of whites agreeing and 92 percent of black respondents agreeing with that statement (Seltzer and Thompson 1985:120). Support for the policy of affirmative action would seem to be as high as for the idea of helping those who have been discriminated against in the past, as 69.2 percent of whites and 85.1 percent of blacks approve of the policy of affirmative action when responding to the following question:

Some large corporations are required to practice what is called affirmative action for Blacks and other minorities. This sometimes requires employers to give special preference to Blacks and other minorities when hiring. Do you approve strongly, approve somewhat, disapprove somewhat or disapprove strongly with affirmative action for Blacks and other minorities? (Seltzer and Thompson 1985:121)

The percentages of both blacks and whites who approve of the same statement about affirmative action for women are nearly identical to the percentages of those who approved of affirmative action for blacks and other minorities, indicating that there seems to be no major split in support for affirmative action directed toward women as opposed to blacks and other minorities as beneficiaries.

When faced with specific implementation of affirmative action programs, however, citizen support for affirmative action begins to fade somewhat. When asked if "businesses should be required to set up special training programs for women, blacks and other minority groups," only 48.9 percent of the white respondents agreed, while 78.4 percent of the black respondents agreed with this statement (Selzer and Thompson 1985:122). Responses to a question about quotas ("unless quotas are used, blacks and other minorities just won't get a fair shake") indicate an even sharper drop in support, with only 39.5 percent of whites and 75.7 percent of blacks agreeing with that statement (Selzer and Thompson 1985:123). These results are similar to those found in other studies indicating that, when the focus changes from abstract questions regarding either equality or affirmative action to specific implementations of affirmative action, support will drop sharply among whites. Seligman summarizes this tendency in American attitudes:

Most educated Americans today would agree that several minorities, and women, suffer from discrimination in employment, that the discrimination is destructive and irrational, and that working to end it is a proper activity for government. Unfortunately, it is not clear what government should do and all too clear that wise policies do not flow naturally from good intentions (Seligman 1973:161).

Lipset and Schneider (1978) contend that Americans are making a distinction in their minds between steps that are "compensatory action" and those that constitute "preferential treatment." According to Lipset and Schneider, this distinction--which can lead to seeming inconsistencies in the responses of Americans to questions about affirmative action--actually involves a conflict between two deeply held American values, those of "individualism" and "egalitarianism." They summarize in regard to affirmative action policies:

> Affirmative action policies, have, of course, forced a sharp confrontation between egalitarian and individualistic values. We have noted that white Americans look favorably upon "compensatory action," since compensation for past discrimination is consistent with the egalitarian creed and essentially makes the conditions of competition "fairer" without violating the notion of a competitive system. But most Americans, including many blacks, oppose the notion of "preferential treatment," since such treatment precisely violates the notion of open and fair individual competition (Lipset and Schneider 1978:44).

Sniderman and Hagen also point out the importance that individualism has as a value in American culture in regard to American attitudes about racial equality. This belief that "anybody can make it, whatever his or her circumstances, if only he or she tries" colors the American understanding of equality and responsibility for their position in life, and explains the resistance that Americans have expressed toward public policies intended to achieve greater racial equality within the larger society (Sniderman and Hagen 1985:117). Steps that are perceived to deviate from the principle of merit and individual achievement are resisted. Several studies indicate that support will fall when selection procedures such as affirmative action are perceived to deviate from merit (Nacoste 1985).

Many authors have contended that affirmative action not only violates our strongly held values regarding individualism and individual achievement, but that individuals who benefit from affirmative action programs are subsequently devalued. It is assumed that those individuals achieve not on the basis of their own merits but only because of the affirmative action programs (see, for example, Sowell 1975). Some few empirical studies have sought to gain understanding as to the extent to which affirmative action causes people to attribute the success and/or failure of minorities and women to affirmative action efforts and not to merit or qualifications. The work of Garcia et al., for example, found that "affirmative action does serve to discount the role of ability in explaining the success of minority group members and augment the lack of ability in explaining their failure" (Garcia et al. 1981:436). These authors seem to be indicating that although affirmative action may provide some increase in the numbers of women and minorities in the work force, it may also do some damage to the self-perception of those who benefit from affirmative action, and/or lead others to wrongly discount the real abilities of minorities and women in the work force.

In many ways the conflicts Americans experience within themselves are reflected in the aggregate inconsistencies noted in their attitudes about affirmative action "micro-level" conflicts discussed earlier. These inconsistencies would seem to be a direct parallel to the "macro-level" dilemma of pursuing compensatory and/or preferential policies in the context of a system of law and public philosophy which gives primacy to equal protection of individual rights. At the heart of the issue of attitudes about affirmative action is the attempted resolution within a liberal society, or within citizens of a liberal society, of a conflict in values involving the maintenance of the primacy of the individual and the legitimate pursuit of self-interest, and the need to control or determine the final distribution of goods in society so that that distribution is in the end more equitable than happenstance would dictate. It seems that Americans resolve this conflict by supporting the abstract idea of equality and the notion of affirmative action in the general sense, but express resistance to specific steps to achieve that equality or to implement affirmative action when the value of individualism and individual achiement is too directly challenged. Examining the attitudes of university faculty with regard to this conflict will be especially interesting, in that that group of people is employed in a highly meritocratic professional system in which achievement and advancement is putatively reflective of merit and interference with that system of academic merit is highly resisted by academics.

Little work has been done that directly addresses the question of faculty attitudes concerning affirmative action. One study conducted by Antonio Sisneros at a single university did address the question of faculty and administrative attitudes about affirmative action. Sisneros found that non-minority supervisors and non-minority department chairpersons and program directors tended to feel that affirmative action provides "excessive" preferential treatment for minority pesons (Sisneros 1984). An important national study adressing the question of faculty attitudes on affirmative action was completed by the Carnegie Foundation for the Advancement of

Teaching (CHE) in 1984. This extensive survey of 5,000 faculty members drawn from a sample of 310 institutions consisted of questions on a wide range of subjects, including several questions probing faculty attitudes on affirmative action issues and policies.

Similar to studies of the public cited above, the faculty respondents to the Carnegie Foundation survey were positive about affirmative action in a general sense. For example, 74.7 percent of the respondents believed in their institution's continued commitment to increasing the number of women and minorities on their faculty, and 58.8 percent of the respondents indicated that they were satisfied with the results of affirmative action at their institutions (CHE 1985:27). In spite of these mildly favorable assessments of affirmative action in the general sense, many participants in the Carnegie study expressed serious reservations about some of the specific ramifications of affirmative action policy. For example, 41.1 percent of those surveyed--including over half of the males (51.3 percent)--felt that affirmative action was unfair to white males (CHE 1985:4). In addition, 88 percent of the respondents were opposed to the relaxation of normal academic requirements in the appointment of minority group faculty members (CHE 1985:24). This finding is not unlike the change in opinions expressed by members of the general public when making the transition from abstract questions about racial equality or affirmative action to specific programs and issues. Support tends to fade as the issues and questions become more complete.

This study provides an important opportunity to increase our understanding of faculty attitudes about affirmative action. An understanding of such attitudes is important as well for a broader understanding of the individualism versus egalitarianism tensions of contemporary postindustrial societies. Faculty are a particularly interesting group to study inasmuch as they have the somewhat unusual capability of making collegial hiring and promotional decisions. Given that their attitudes about affirmative action are likely to have been put to the test of making hiring and promotion decisions in recent years, the attitudes of faculty are likely to reflect well-reasoned viewpoints on the matter of affirmative action in the academy. Through this study we will be able to ask: How do our most educated professionals within a liberal society resolve the macro and micro conflicts inherent in a policy such as affirmative action? Do individuals respond to affirmative action primarily from the ethic of individualism, self-interest and faith in meritocratic fairness, or do they instead base their views on what they think the public interest requires for the achievement of social equity?

3

Affirmative Action
and the Law

This chapter will set forth an overview of developments in the statutory, administrative and judicial specification of the operational meaning of affirmative action. This affirmative action policy, which constrains the admissions and personnel recruitment, tenure and promotions decisions of higher education, is shaped by the official actions and authoritative interpretations from all three branches of government. This chapter will outline the legal roots of affirmative action in both the civil rights legislation enacted by Congress and in the executive orders issued by several presidents. Judicial decisions relating to affirmative action, especially affirmative action and higher education, will be outlined next. All three branches of government have contributed to the development of this policy area, and their respective contributions to the overall operation of compensatory justice mechanisms intended to promote greater social equity reflect the complex mix of political, partisan, legal and philosophical considerations that come into play in the pluralistic setting of U.S. politics.

CONGRESS

A chief law passed by Congress that relates to affirmative action is the Civil Rights Act of 1964 (42 U.S.C. Section 2000e et. seq.). Two sections of this Act, Title VI and Title VII, are especially relevant to this policy area. Title VI prohibits discrimination on the basis of race, sex or national origin in public accomodations and in federally assisted programs. Title VII of the 1964 act prohibits discrimination by employers or unions, whether public or private. It should be noted that this Act, in contrast to the logic expressed by the Commission on Civil Rights for affirmative action in the introduction, focuses only on the elimination of barriers. It is not intended to compensate for the effects of past discrimination, but only to remove currently existing barriers based on race, sex or national origin. Section 703(j) 78 Stat. 255 as amended 86 Stat. 109, 42 U.S.C. ss2000e-2(a) provides:

> Nothing contained in this title shall be interpreted to require any employer . . . to grant preferential treatment to any individual or to any group because of the race, color, religion, sex or national origin of such individual or group on account of an imbalance which may exist with respect to the total number or percentage of persons of any race, color, religion, sex, or national origin employed by any employer.

Much later, Alan Bakke would use Title VII as the basis of his reverse discrimination suit brought against the University California, Davis, which is described later in this chapter.

A second law relevant to the policy area of affirmative action is the 1972 Equal Employment Opportunity Act. This Act gave the Equal Employment Opportunity Commission (EEOC) stronger enforcement mechanisms through the issuance of cease and desist orders. The 1972 Act also brought the Office of Federal Contract Compliance, previously contained within the Department of Labor, to the EEOC. The Commission's jurisdiction was broadened to include state and local government employees and employees of educational institutions. The 1972 Act also gave to the EEOC some powers over federal employees, taking away the Civil Service Commission's ability to handle discrimination complaints within the Civil Service (P.L. 92-261).

These two key statutes have provided the groundwork for the empowerment of administrative enforcement agencies such as the U.S. Commission on Civil Rights and the Equal Employment Opportunity Commission, which continue to oversee regulations and official interpretations of affirmative action policy. A brief discussion of the roles of these agencies will be included in the following section on the contributions and functions of the executive branch in the development of affirmative action.

THE EXECUTIVE BRANCH

Presidential executive orders constitute a chief source of the authority and language of affirmative action--both historically speaking and in terms of current practice. In addition, agencies of the executive branch have developed administrative compliance regulations pertinent to affirmative action which have the force of law for all intents and purposes. Some of the more important executive orders and administrative regulations pertinent to affirmative action in higher education are described below.

Of the several executive orders relating to the development of affirmative action, Lyndon Johnson's 1964 executive order no. 11246 (32 Fed. Reg. 12319) is by far the most important. That order (still in force) "prohibits federal contract funds from going to employers who discriminate in their employment policies or practices on the basis of race, color, religion, or national origin." In 1968 the order was amended to include sex discrimination by executive order 11375 (32 Fed. Reg. 14303).

The EEOC, given its greater enforcement powers obtained through the 1972 Equal Employment Opportunity Act, coordinates the issuance of regulations and requirements that control the implementation of affirmative action policy by recipients of federal funds. Recipients of federal money, including universities, are subject to the requirements set down by these agencies. Failure to comply with federal guidelines could result in the loss of federal money, hence these regulations remain a very important part of affirmative action policy for universities.

For example, the following statement--replete with references to statutes, executive orders and administrative regulations--constitutes a translation of these affirmative action policies to the operating policies of Washington State University:

> It is the policy of Washington State University to prohibit and eliminate discrimination on grounds of race, color, national origin, sex, or religion and to provide equal employment for all, pursuant to the Federal Executive Orders, 11246 and 11375, as amended. . . . Moreover the policy also adheres to other federal and state laws . . . the State Equal Rights Amendment, Title VI of the Civil Rights Act of 1964; Title VII of the Civil Rights Act of 1964 . . . which guarantee equal opportunity and equal employment

opportunity to individuals and groups within our society (*Bulletin/Calendar* 1979:3).

THE JUDICIAL SYSTEM

The judicial system of the United States has played a major role in the way that affirmative action as a public policy has been developed and implemented. Several important cases dealing with affirmative action and its implementation have been heard by the U.S. Supreme Court, and its decisions in those cases have had great impact on the way in which affirmative action is put into practice by regulatory agencies, public sector employers and private institutions of all kinds. This chapter will outline briefly some of the more important cases that have addressed the constitutionality of affirmative action in general, and two major cases that dealt with affirmative action in higher education specifically. The conflict of values discussed in the previous chapter is reflected in the reasoning of the Supreme Court as it has attempted to balance the guarantee of procedural fairness for non-minorities with the legitimate need to redress past discrimination and to enhance equity in educational and employment opportunity. Commentary on the final meaning and long-term impacts of these decisions for higher education is rather mixed, reflecting the great difficulties to be overcome in bringing more women and minorities into the work force while preserving the meritocratic systems so dear to the liberal heart.

Many of the familiar aspects of affirmative action as it is implemented today were derived from the landmark case of *Griggs v. Duke Power Company* [401 U.S. 424 (1971)]. In this case the Supreme Court invalidated testing for employment that disproportionately excluded minorities if those tests were not provably job related and if their use did not constitute a compelling "business necessity" (U.S. Civil Rights Commission 1979:179). "Concrete remedies" to employment practices that have discriminatory effects that have developed from *Griggs* include: (1) the substitution of word-of-mouth recruiting with recruiting specifically designed to target and recruit underutilized minorities; (2) the elimination of eligibility lists drawn from unvalidated tests and other standards that have discriminatory effects; and (3) the institution of training programs by unions and employers for minority applicants (U.S. Civil Rights Commisson 1979:181).

The ultimate effect of the *Griggs* decision was to allow programs implemented by employers involving preferential affirmative action on behalf of women and minorities. The court found that these necessarily preferential personnel practices

benefiting women and minorities were violative of neither the equal protection clause of the Fourteenth Amendment nor the strictures against preferential consideration stated in Title VII.
A similar decision was reached in *U.S. Steelworkers of America v. Weber* [443 U.S. 193 (1979)] in which an affirmative action plan involving training opportunities for black employees of the Kaiser Aluminum and Chemical Corporation was upheld. Weber challenged this plan with the claim that it violated the provisions of sections 703 (a) and (d) of Title VII of the Civil Rights Act of 1964 which makes it "unlawful to discriminate on the basis of race." In its decision, the court made reference to the legislative history and intent of Title VII of the 1964 Civil Rights Act. Justice Brennan, writing for the court, said:

> Examination of these sources [the legislative history of Title VII and the historical context from which the Act arose] makes clear that an interpretation of the sections that forbade all race-conscious affirmative action would "bring about an end completely at variance with the purpose of the statute" and must be rejected (*U.S. Steelworkers of America v. Weber* [443 U.S. 193, 202 (1979)]).

The court upheld the existence of voluntarily undertaken affirmative action plans in the private sector, noting in regard to the contention that affirmative action plans violated Title VII protections for non-minorities:

> It would be ironic indeed if a law triggered by a Nation's concern over centuries of racial injustice and intended to improve the lot of those who had "been excluded from the American dream for so long" [110 Cong. Rec. 6552 (1964) (remarks of Sen. Humphrey)], constituted the first legislative prohibition of all voluntary, private, race-conscious efforts to abolish traditional patterns of racial segregation and hierarchy (*U.S. Steelworkers of America v. Weber* [443 U.S. 193, 204 (1979)]).

A similar approval of affirmative action programs was made by the Court in *Fullilove et al. v. Klutznick, Secretary of Commerce* [448 U.S. 448 (1980)], in which a set-aside program for minority contractors was upheld. In this case the petitioners challenged that the Minority Business Enterprise (MBE) provision of the Public Works Employment Act of 1977--"in which 10 percent of federal funds granted for local public works projects must be used by the state and local grantee to procure services or supplies from businesses owned by minority group members"--violated the Equal Protection Clause of the Fourteenth Amendment and the equal treatment component of the Due Process Clause of the Fifth Amendment [448 U.S. 448, 448 (1980)]. The court upheld the constitutionality of this program, finding that the MBE program was within the scope of Congress' power:

> Congress, after due consideration, perceived a pressing need to move forward with new approaches in the continuing effort to achieve the goal of equality of economic opportunity. In this effort, Congress has necessary latitude to try new techniques such as the limited use of racial and ethnic criteria to accomplish remedial objectives (*Fullilove v. Klutznick* [448 U.S. 448, 490 (1980)]).

The court also rejected claims that the MBE program was unconstitutional because it prohibited some non-minority contractors from the program. Chief Justice Burger, writing for the court, argued:

> It is not a constitutional defect in this program that it may disappoint the expectations of non-minority firms. When effectuating a limited and properly tailored remedy to cure the effects of prior discrimination, such a "sharing of the burden" by innocent parties is not impermissible (*Fullilove v. Klutznick* [448 U.S. 448, 484 (1980)]).

A recent case, however, in which an MBE set-aside plan adopted by the city of Richmond was struck down, indicated that the court is willing to find affirmative action plans unconstitutional if they fail to meet the "strict scrutiny" requirements of "a compelling governmental interest justifying the plan" and a set-aside plan "narrowly tailored to accomplish a remedial purpose" [*City of Richmond v. J.A. Croson Company U.S.* (1989)].

The extent to which the burden imposed on non-minorities is too high in regard to the implementation of affirmative action programs was addressed in the 1986 case of *Wygant et al. v. Jackson Board of Education et al.* [476 U.S. 267 (1986)]. In this case, a lay-off plan adopted by the Jackson Board of Education--in which seniority in laying-off personnel could be bypassed such that "at no time would there be a greater percentage of minority personnel laid off than the current percentage of minority personnel employed at the time of the layoff" (*Wygant v. Jackson* [476 U.S. 267 (1986)])--was struck down as a violation of the Equal Protection Clause. Although the court reasserted that affirmative action programs were allowable under some circumstances, it nonetheless opined that

> We have recognized, however, that in order to remedy the effects of prior discrimination, it may be necessary to take race into account. As part of this Nation's dedication to eradicating racial discrimination, innocent persons may be called upon to bear some of the burden of the remedy (*Wygant v. Jackson* [476 U.S. 267, 280-281 (1986)]).

This program, however, imposed burdens the court considered too great. The court distinguished between the burden imposed by hiring goals and layoffs:

> layoffs impose the entire burden of achieving racial equality on particular individuals, often resulting in serious disruption of their lives. That burden is too intrusive. We therefore hold that, as a means of accomplishing purposes that otherwise might be legitimate, the Board's layoff plan is not sufficiently narrowly tailored (*Wygant v. Jackson* [476 U.S. 267, 283 (1986)]).

The burden imposed by the lay-off plan on non-minorities was too great. In this instance, the competing goals of protecting non-minority individuals and achieving greater racial equality resulted in a decision that favored the protection of the non-minorities' interests.

A further step in the direction of protecting the interests of non-minority members was taken by the court in *Martin et al. v. Wilks et al.* [U.S. (1989)]. In this case the Supreme Court allowed white firefighters in Birmingham, Alabama to challenge employment practices intended to promote black firefighters that were the result of consent decrees entered into by the city. The white firefighters claimed that the promotion of black firefighters over more qualified white firefighters in accordance with the consent decree constituted "impermissible racial discrimination in violation of the Constitution and federal statute." The Supreme Court ruled to allow the white firefighters to challenge the employment practices because they were not party to the consent decrees entered into by the city. This decision may open up other affirmative action plans created as a result of consent decrees to attack by non minorities not party to those decisions.

In yet another 1989 decision, *Wards Cove Packing Co. Inc. et al. v. Atonio et al.* [U.S. (1989)], the Supreme Court further opened affirmative action programs to attack. In this case the court overturned a Court of Appeals decision in which a cannery's employment practices were found to have a "disparate impact" on minorities. Specifically, the Court found that calculating "disparate impact" on minorities by comparing the percentage of non-white and white workers unacceptable, and placed the burden of proof in determining disparate impact on those bringing suit. Justice White wrote in the majority opinion:

> any employer who had a segment of his workforce that was--for some reason--racially imbalanced, could be haled into court and forced to engage in the expensive and time-consuming task of defending the "business necessity" of the methods used to select the other members of his workforce (*Wards Cove Packing Co. Inc. et al. v. Atonio et al.* [U.S. No. 87-1387, slip op. at 8 (1989)]).

The totality of the impact of this decision on affirmative action and civil rights can be assessed in the opening paragraph of Justice Blackmun's dissent:

> Today a bare majority of the Court takes three major strides backwards in the battle against racial discrimination. It reaches out to make last term's plurality opinion in *Watson v. Fort Worth Bank and Trust,* 487 U.S. -(1988), the law, thereby upsetting the longstanding distribution of burdens of proof in Title VII disparate impact cases. It bars the use of internal workforce comparisons in the making of a prima facie case of discrimination, even where the structure of industry in question renders any other statistical comparision meaningless. And it requires practice-by-practice statistical proof of causation, even where, as here, such proof would be impossible (*Wards Cove Packing Co. Inc. et al. v. Atonio et al.* [U.S. No. 87-1387, slip op. at 1 (1989)]).

The influence of the Reagan appointees on the court may lead to further changes in the case law affecting affirmative action in the future. This new majority on the court seems likely to continue to balance the competing goals of protecting non minority individuals and achieving greater racial equality by deciding on behalf of protecting non-minorities.

John Nalbandian, in an excellent recent (1989) review of the Supreme Court's opinions and reasoning in cases dealing with affirmative action, concludes that the use of affirmative action programs and procedures has become accepted as part of the fixed and established law by the Supreme Court Justices. He is joined in this view by some (Waldo and Davison 1987), while others would disagree and claim a serious elimination of federal court protection of the interests of the beneficiaries of affirmative action (Rasnic 1988). Nalbandian quotes Justice O'Connor in saying that "remedying past or present racial discrimination by a state actor is a sufficiently weighty state interest to warrant the remedial use of a carefully constructed affirmative action program" (Nalbandian 1989:39). Nalbandian contends that the Supreme Court has attempted to balance several competing values in its decisions regarding affirmative action. A chief value to be protected is, of course, individual rights, particularly the individual rights of non-minorities who may suffer from the implementation of affirmative action programs. The court is still searching for a means by which adverse effects on non-minorities who were not directly responsible for the adverse effects can be afforded adequate protection within a general policy of high tolerance for established gender- and race-conscious preferential practices. Nalbandian notes the reluctance of the court to allow preferential programs that adversely affect non-minorities; when "carefully crafted" and "well-justified" preferential policies are involved, the court has sustained the affirmative action measures quite consistently (Nalbandian 1989:40-41).

Nalbandian argues that "the key task of balancing the interests of minority victims and innocent nonminorities fundamentally revolves around questions of individual rights" (Nalbandian 1989:41). A second value that the Supreme Court has attempted to take into consideration in decisions involving affirmative action, according to Nalbandian, is that of social equity or distributive justice. This value usually entails some sort of compensatory action to remedy past wrongs. Nalbandian points out that this value "results in fair treatment of people as members of a class rather than as individuals" (Nalbandian 1989:41). A final value taken into consideration by the court is that of efficiency, or the concern for such qualifications as knowledge and skill of applicants. According to Nalbandian, it is this aspect of merit, or dealing with the day-to-day world of personnel management in a meritocratic system, that the Supreme Court has not dealt with adequately. He suggests that employee perceptions of "unfair preferential treatment" received by minorities may be due to the lack of attention paid to the value of efficiency by the Supreme Court in their decisions (Nalbandian 1989:44). He contends that future Supreme Court decisions dealing with affirmative action will need to take this value of efficiency into account more fully (Nalbandian 1989:43).

Nalbandian's description of the conflict of values inherent in the Supreme Court's decisions is similar to the conflict of values concerning affirmative action discussed in the previous chapter. The Supreme Court, acting as the final arbiter of our society's major legal (and value) conflicts, reasons out for all of us how to balance the needs of individuals--and the protection of their rights--with the need for equity in the final distribution of goods in our society. It is as de Tocqueville noted; Americans eventually take all of their major conflicts to the judicial system for final resolution. In the case of affirmative action, the Supreme Court has attempted to resolve the conflict of competing values by allowing affirmative action programs within certain justifications and conditions of need.

Since, as Nalbandian notes, affirmative action has now become a permanent institutionalized aspect of personnel practices in this country (1989:43), many institutions have voluntarily established affirmative action programs in order to ensure movement toward the goal of equity in their respective work force. Institutions of higher education were among the first to voluntarily undertake various steps to create affirmative action programs. Two important Supreme Court cases addressing affirmative action involved universities, and those cases brought to the surface some of the more difficult and perhaps unresolvable issues involved in this public policy. These two cases are *DeFunis v. Odegaard and the University of Washington* [416 U.S. 312 (1974)], and *Regents of the University of California v. Bakke* [438 U.S. 265 (1978)].

It is significant that both of these cases took place at universities, and both involved challenges to the meritocratic system that were created by those universities' attempts to increase minority representation in their professional schools. The large degree to which admission to and progress within higher education in this country is based on merit brings to the surface the conflicts inherent in affirmative action, a policy that in its implementation can involve challenges to the exclusive use of merit to decide among competing individuals seeking access to limited spaces in public institutions of higher learning. As Ralph Rossum points out, the extent to which higher education places a premium on merit, standards and individual achievement makes the university a difficult setting in which to practice preferential selection (Rossum 1980:2). In both *DeFunis* and *Bakke*, private suit was brought by a white male applicant who was rejected by a public institution's professional school. Both men were objecting to the school's voluntarily adopted use of racial categories to "admit less qualified minority students on a preferential basis" (Sindler 1978:2). Both DeFunis and Bakke claimed that they had been deprived of equal protection under the Fourteenth Amendment because the schools had racially classified applicants (Sindler 1978:2). Bakke claimed as well that the admissions program at the University of California at Davis, where he was attempting to gain entrance to medical school, was in violation of Title VI of the Civil Rights Act of 1964, "which provided that no program receiving federal aid shall exclude, deny benefits to, or subject to discrimination, 'anyone on the grounds of race'" (Mooney 1982:4).

The *DeFunis* case, although heard by the U.S. Supreme Court, was never decided. The Justices decided that the case was moot given DeFunis's pending completion of his legal studies at the University of Washington--the question of his admittance to the program was no longer relevant. In the *Bakke* case, however, the decision was handed down in June 1978. The court was severely divided in its opinons about the *Bakke* case, resulting in a confusing mixture of agreement on some issues and disagreement on many others. Wayne McCormack summarizes two points on which there is some clarity:

(1) In public institutions subject to Title VI, a two-track admission program in which a specific number of seats is reserved exclusively for applicants from designated minority groups is impermissible in the absence of appropriate legislative, judicial or administrative findings; (2) A properly constructed race-conscious admission program is legally permissible under certain circumstances (McCormack 1978:1).

Summaries and commentary on the *Bakke* decision are mixed in their assessment of the meaning of the opinions of the Justices. The Commission on Civil Rights finds that the decision gives legitimacy to programs of affirmative action (U.S. Civil Rights Commission 1979), but others have been less optimistic about the final impact of the *Bakke* decision for minorities and women in higher education. Merline Pitre divides scholars who have analyzed the impact of *Bakke* on higher education and the welfare of minorities into three categories. In the first category are scholars who argue that it is not the duty of the state to remedy past wrongs through programs such as affirmative action. In the second category are those scholars who contend that it is indeed the duty of the state to remedy past societal discrimination. The final category that Pitre creates contains those scholars who claim that the Court's decision was confusing and vague in *Bakke* and is in the end an "accommodative approach between the real and the ideal" (Pitre 1981:83). This categorization of the commentary on affirmative action reflects the spectrum of approaches to a policy such as affirmative action that reach from the uncompromising protection of non minority individual rights to the advocation of state activity to ensure a more equitable final distribution of employment. In the middle of this debate is the Supreme Court's decision on *Bakke*.

Pitre classifies Archibald Cox in the middle "accomodationist" category, and notes that it was his contention "that Powell [in *Bakke*] sought accommodation between the ideal of an equality blind to race and color and the social need for affirmative action" (Pitre 1981:84). The confusing set of arguments and opinions finally handed down by a 5-4 split court has already been noted above. In many ways the decision represents a compromise between competing values. Jonathan Cole notes that it is a "problematic" of affirmative action that it represents the "competition between affirmative action and older principles of equality of opportunity; the relationship between principles of individual and group justice" (Cole 1979:261). The court's decision in *Bakke* is an attempt, however muddled, to balance those competing values.

Although the balance attempted by the court in the *Bakke* decision may be viewed optimistically by some, many other commentators are less encouraged. Gerald Gill, for example, claims that the *Bakke* decision has led to the dismantling of minority admissions programs at many universities, and has encouraged opponents of affirmative action to criticize the remaining minority admissions programs as being in violation of the *Bakke* decision (Gill 1980:68). Michael Woodard, in reference to recent judicial and executive decisions, claims that they "appear to reflect a pattern of consistently legitimizing the idea of reverse discrimination and providing a compromised interpretation of the affirmative action concept" (Woodard 1982:173). Pitre cites the argument of Eric Lincoln in saying that "because of vagueness and lack of unanimity by the Court . . . wherever affirmative action has been inconvenient, disruptive, or simply undesireable, the Bakke decision will be read as a permission if not an obligation to reconsider" (Pitre 1981:84).

In summary, affirmative action has been upheld by the Supreme Court in its rulings, but it is held within some serious limitations. Affirmative action programs that meet certain requirements of proven past discrimination and that minimize the adverse impacts on non-minorities are considered acceptable by the Supreme Court as a way to rectify the impact of past disadvantage suffered by minorities and women. The court's conditional support of affirmative action programs has held fast through recent decisions such as *Johnson v. Transportation Agency Santa Clara County, California* (1987). To some observers and scholars, however, the Court dealt affirmative action a serious blow in the *Bakke* decision. Some such writers point to the fact that institutions wishing to avoid the use of affirmative action policies may now do so with less fear of adverse reaction as a result of *Bakke*. Most scholars, however, focus instead on the fact that affirmative action programs have been approved "in principle" repeatedly by the court, and that preferential programs in instances of serious underutilization of minorities are highly likely to be sustained and protected in federal courts.

Higher education has had difficulty with the policy of affirmative action because of fears of damage to the system of meritocracy on which both admissions and faculty personnel systems are supposed to rest. Frank and Mintz, in their assessment of the impact of recent Supreme Court decisions on affirmative action in higher education, point out that the court approved the "consideration of affirmative action factors in the evaluation of qualified applicants" (Frank and Mintz 1987:59). They further write:

> The Court's ruling in *Johnson* is of obvious significance for higher education, where many institutions have established voluntary affirmative action programs to increase the representation of women and minority group members in their faculty ranks. It confirms AAUP's position opposing quotas but supporting the affirmative consideration of sex or race in an appointment decision (Frank and Mintz 1987:60).

Here again we see the need to balance the competing values of acting affirmatively to achieve a more representative work force and protecting individual rights through selection and promotion based on merit. The American Association of University Professors (AAUP) stops short of advocating the compromise of merit implied in the use of quotas, but is supportive of the principle of acting affirmatively to increase the number of women and minorities in higher education. There is no question that the policy of affirmative action has been supported by the Supreme Court and that it has become an entrenched part of personnel practices, as noted by Nalbandian (1989). How this policy is perceived by and dealt with by members of university faculties is the subject of the next section of this study.

4

Data and Methods

The data for this study were collected in 1986 by the Fellows of the Interdisciplinary Research Center for Faculty Stress and Productivity at Washington State University. This research was made possible by a grant from the W.W. Kellogg Foundation and the Office of Grants and Research Development at Washington State University. The 1986 study is based on a previous National Faculty Stress Study conducted in 1982 by Walt Gmelch, Nicholas Lovrich and Phyllis Kaye Wilke. Gmelch, Lovrich and Wilke developed their sample by selecting at random forty public and forty private universities from among all American universities that offer comprehensive doctoral degree programs. They drew a sample of 1,920 faculty from the college catalogs of these institutions, stratified so that they included equal numbers from public and private institutions, equal proportions of assistant, associate and full professors, and finally equal proportions from each of eight Biglan disciplinary clusters.[1]

The National Faculty Stress Survey questionnaire asked respondents about their perceptions of job-related stress within the college and university work environment. From this study Gmelch, Lovrich and Wilke were able to develop several scales relating to the stress faculty experienced in their work environment.[2] The second National Faculty Stress Study conducted in 1986 focused on gender and race issues. A different sample selection method was used to ensure that adequate numbers of both women and minority scholars would be included in the final sample. New sections of questions were added to the second national study questionaire. The 1986 National Faculty Stress Study contains the same stress scales contained in the 1982 study, but added a new section of questions that asked respondents about their views toward the affirmative action programs on their own college and university campuses. A more detailed explanation of these new questions will follow later in this chapter.

SAMPLE COLLECTION FOR THE 1986 NATIONAL FACULTY STRESS STUDY

To ensure an adequate representation of black faculty, all major organizations representing the academic disciplines (for example, the American Political Science Association) were asked to share their lists of minority members with the researchers. Assistance was also received in locating black faculty from affirmative action officers and Ethnic Studies Departments nationwide. In addition, letters were sent to eminent black scholars asking them for names of their black colleagues and other black scholars within the broader academic community of their respective disciplines or areas of study. The overall cooperation of both institutions and individuals was very positive. To be included in the sample, all scholars had to have earned either the Ed.D. or Ph.D. degree, and be employed fulltime as a member of the instructional faculty at their institution.

Once the list of black faculty had been collected, each black female was matched to a white female, and each black male was matched to two white males and one white female using their respective college catalogs. The matching process at this stage was done by matching tenure status and discipline, using Biglan's categorization of the disciplines (see Note 1). A total sample of 2,095 college and university faculty was drawn from 233 colleges and universities. Responses were received from faculty at 193 institutions (see Figure 4.1 for a complete listing of respondent institutions). The Dillman (1978) "total design method" was employed in the mailing and collection of the mail surveys and a response rate of over 50 percent from the original sample was achieved. Given the length of the survey and time constraints of university faculty, this response rate was quite satisfactory. For a more detailed account of the representativeness of the sample see the discussion presented in Smith and Witt (forthcoming).

Figure 4.1
National Faculty Stress Study Respondent's
Universities Categorized by Carnegie Ranking

1.1 Case Western Reserve
    University
1.1 Columbia University
1.1 Cornell University
1.1 Duke University
1.1 Harvard University
1.1 Johns Hopkins University
1.1 Massachusetts Institute of
    Technology
1.1 Michigan State University
1.1 New York University
1.1 North Carolina State University
1.1 Northwestern University
1.1 Ohio State University
1.1 Pennsylvania State University
1.1 Princeton University
1.1 Purdue University
1.1 Rutgers University
1.1 San Diego State University
1.1 Stanford University
1.1 Texas A&M University
1.1 University of Arizona
1.1 University of California
    Berkeley
1.1 University of California
    Davis
1.1 University of California Los
    Angeles
1.1 University of Colorado
1.1 University of Florida
1.1 University of Georgia
1.1 University of Illinois-Urbana
1.1 University of Kentucky
1.1 University of Maryland
1.1 University of Michigan
1.1 University of Minnesota
1.1 University of Mississippi
1.1 University of Missouri
1.1 University of North Carolina
1.1 University of Pennsylvania
1.1 University of Pittsburgh
1.1 University of Rochester
1.1 University of San Diego

1.1 University of Tennessee
1.1 University of Texas
1.1 University of Utah
1.1 University of Washington
1.1 Vanderbilt University
1.1 Washington University
1.1 Yale University

1.2 Boston University
1.2 Brown University
1.2 Carnegie-Mellon University
1.2 Claremont Graduate School
1.2 Colorado State University
1.2 Emory University
1.2 Florida State University
1.2 Illinois Institute of Technology
1.2 Indiana University Bloomington
1.2 Louisiana State University
1.2 Oklahoma State University
1.2 Rice University
1.2 SUNY-Buffalo
1.2 Syracuse University
1.2 Temple University
1.2 Tufts University
1.2 Tulane Medical Center
1.2 University of Chicago
1.2 University of Connecticut
1.2 University of Massachusetts
    Amherst
1.2 University of Nebraska
1.2 University of Oklahoma
1.2 University of Virginia
1.2 Virginia Polytechnical
    Institute
1.2 Washington State University
1.2 Wayne State University
1.2 West Virginia University

1.3 Albany College
1.3 Arizona State University
1.3 Boston College
1.3 Dartmouth University
1.3 Drexel University

Figure 4.1 (Continued)

1.3 Georgetown University
1.3 Kent State University
1.3 Loyola University-Chicago
1.3 Northeastern University
1.3 Southern Illinois University
1.3 SUNY-Albany
1.3 SUNY-Stoney Brook
1.3 University of Alabama
1.3 University of California
    Irvine
1.3 University of California
    Riverside
1.3 University of California
    Santa Barbara
1.3 University of Delaware
1.3 University of Houston
1.3 University of Idaho
1.3 University of Louisville
1.3 University of Notre Dame
1.3 University of Southern
    Mississippi
1.3 University of Wyoming

1.4 Clark College
1.4 Georgia State University
1.4 Memphis State University
1.4 Miami University
1.4 North Texas State University
1.4 Northern Illinois University
1.4 Southern Methodist   University
1.4 Texas Technological Institute
1.4 University of Wisconsin
    Milwaukee
1.4 Virginia Commonwealth
    University

2.1 Bradley University
2.1 California State Polytechnic
    University
2.1 California State University-
    Fullerton
2.1 California State University-
    Hayward
2.1 California State University-
    Sacramento

2.1 Central State University
    (Ohio)
2.1 Creighton University
2.1 DePaul University
2.1 Eastern Illinois University
2.1 Eastern New Mexico University
2.1 Eastern Washington University
2.1 Florida A & M
2.1 Gonzaga University
2.1 Hampton Institute
2.1 Indiana State University
2.1 Jackson State University
2.1 Lincoln University
2.1 McNeese State University
2.1 Mississippi Valley State
    University
2.1 Morgan State University
2.1 Norfolk State College
2.1 North Carolina A&T
2.1 North Carolina Central
    University
2.1 Old Dominion University
2.1 Portland State University
2.1 Prairie View A&M
2.1 Rhode Island College
2.1 Rochester Institute of
    Technology
2.1 Seton Hall
2.1 Simmons College
2.1 Southern University/A&M
    College
2.1 Southwest Texas State
2.1 SUNY-Binghamton
2.1 SUNY-Brockport
2.1 Tennessee State University
2.1 Trenton State College
2.1 Trinity University
2.1 Union College
2.1 University of Nevada Las
    Vegas
2.1 University of San Francisco
2.1 University of Southern
    Florida
2.1 Virginia State College
2.1 Wake Forest University

Figure 4.1 (Continued)

2.1 Westchester State University
2.1 Western Illinois University
2.1 Wright State University
2.1 Xavier University

2.2 Coppin State College
2.2 Fayetteville State University
2.2 Glassboro State University
2.2 Jersey State College
2.2 Longwood College
2.2 Springfield College
2.2 St. Olaf College
2.2 Winston-Salem College

3.1 Amherst College
3.1 Bowdoin College
3.1 Carleton College
3.1 Chatham College
3.1 Colgate University
3.1 Connecticutt College
3.1 Grinnel University
3.1 Haverford College
3.1 Hobart and William Smith
     College
3.1 Pomona College
3.1 Sarah Lawrence University
3.1 Smith College
3.1 Swarthmore College
3.1 Wesleyan University
3.1 Wheaton College

3.2 Atlanta University
3.2 Augsburg College
3.2 California State University-
     Bakersfield
3.2 Colby College
3.2 Dillard University
3.2 Fisk University
3.2 Hampshire College
3.2 Johnson C. Smith College
3.2 Knoxville College
3.2 Luther College
3.2 Morris Brown College
3.2 Otterbein College
3.2 Queens College
3.2 Wilkes-Barre College

4.0 Bennett College
4.0 College of Alameda
4.0 Community College of
     Allegheny
4.0 Holy Cross University
4.0 Nassau Community College
4.0 University of North Florida

5.1 Colgate-Rochester Divinity
     School
5.1 Union Theological Seminary
5.2 University of San Francisco
5.5 CUNY Baruch College
5.8 Bank Street College
5.9 CUNY John Jay College

The study sample reported here is a matched sample taken from the aggregate sample of the 1986 study. This matched sample consists of 246 matched pairs of faculty, yielding a total sample of 492 individual faculty subjects. The matched sample was developed by "hand matching" respondents on the basis of tenure status, age, marital status, academic discipline, Carnegie ranking of institution at which they are working, gender and ethnicity. Tables 4.1 through 4.5 display the questionnaire breakdown of the study respondents on each of the variables used to create the matched sample. Given the development of a sample including proportional numbers of minorities and women, the sample differs from the national averages in terms of its ethnic and gender makeup. A further difference can

Table 4.1
Breakdown of Marital Status of National Faculty Stress Study Respondents

	White Respondents	Black Respondents
Single	(58) 25%	(84) 35%
Married	(178) 75%	(153) 65%
Total	(236)	(237)

Table 4.2
Breakdown of National Faculty Stress Study Respondents by Sex Compared to National Average

	N.F.S.S. Sample		National Average
	White Respondents	Black Respondents	
Male	(150) 63%	(150) 63%	70%
Female	(87) 37%	(88) 37%	30%
Total	237*	238	

Note: National average information compiled from Bowen and Schuster (1986:57), and includes full-time and part-time faculty.

* One case was "missing"

Table 4.3
Ethnicity of National Faculty Stress Study Respondents
Compared to National Averages

	N.F.S.S. Sample	National Averages
White (non-minority)	48.4% (232)	91.9%
Black	50% (236)	1.3%
Native American	0% (0)	0.3%
Hispanic	0.4% (1)	0.8%
Asian	0.8% (2)	5.7%
Other	0.4% (1)	

Notes: National averages compiled from Bowen and Schuster (1986:59). National average numbers are for persons in the sciences, social sciences and engineering only.

be found in the number of lecturers and instructors included in the National Faculty Stress Study sample. Very few lecturers and instructors are included in the National Faculty Stress Study. Because of the peculiarities of this matching process, some respondents were dropped from the matched pairs sample because an accurate match for them could not be found. The hand-matching process, although time- and labor-intensive, provides data from matched pairs which are relatively rare. Matching on the above dimensions allows for control not available in the original sample. William Hays notes: "The factor or factors used to match pairs is less likely to be responsible for any observed difference in the groups than if two unmatched groups were used" (1973:424).

Table 4.4
Breakdown of National Faculty Stress Study
Respondents by Age

	White Respondents	Black Respondents
First Quartile Cutoff	36	36
Second Quartile Cutoff	41	42
Third Quartile Cutoff	49	50
Fourth Quartile Cutoff	+49	+50

Note: The mean age for white respondents = 42.95.
The mean age for black respondents = 42.11.

Table 4.5
Academic Rank of National Faculty Stress Study
Respondents Compared to National Averages

	N.F.S.S. Sample		National Averages
Rank	White	Black	Total
Instructor/Lecturer	(7) 2.9%	(6) 2.5%	24.6%
Assistant Professor	(67) 28.2%	(69) 29.0%	23.9%
Associate Professor	(92) 38.7%	(91) 38.2%	24.5%
Professor	(71) 29.8%	(71) 29.8%	27.0%

Note: National averages compiled from Bowen and Schuster
(1986:44). National Faculty Stress data compiled by the author.

VARIABLES ADDRESSING AFFIRMATIVE ACTION ISSUES

The 1986 National Faculty Stress Study contained a series of questions addressing "attitudes on contemporary university issues." The survey respondents were given the following preface, and then asked to complete questions that dealt with general impacts of affirmative action on their own career, their own university and American universities in general:

> In recent years American universities have made considerable effort to bring women and minorities more fully into the mainstream of faculty life. Although few would object to this goal as a general proposition, many have expressed concern over the means employed to accomplish this goal, and over the consequences of those means for faculty members--male and female, minority and nonminority alike. The following section contains several questions pertaining to your views on such issues.

Two questions dealt with respondents' perceptions of the impact of affirmative action on American universities in general. The questions were split such that one question asked respondents to assess the impact on American universities of efforts to promote opportunities for greater employment of racial minorities, and the other question asked respondents to assess the impact on American universities of "efforts to promote opportunities for greater employment of women" on the faculty.[3] Two additional questions asked respondents to assess the impact of university affirmative action programs on both their career and their university.[4]

The National Faculty Stress Study also contained two questions assessing faculty beliefs about two often suggested reasons for the "ill-advised" nature of affirmative action given by opponents to the policy. These questions were preceded by the following preface:

> It has been argued that affirmative action programs for minorities and women are ill-advised for two important reasons: a) they perpetuate the idea that these groups require "extra help" to compensate for supposed inadequacies, and b) they rob the successful, deserving minorities and women of a clear sense of accomplishment. What do you believe about these two points?

Respondents then indicated the extent of their agreement or disagreement to the two reasons contained in the preface above.[5] A final set of questions relating to contemporary university issues asked respondents to indicate whether it was a disadvantage, advantage or made no difference to be minority or female with regard to a series of fifteen career dimensions relevant to academic career progress. Respondents answered separately for minority scholars and women scholars.[6] The career dimension questions were prefaced by the following:

> While some argue that serious barriers continue to exist for minority and women scholars in the university, others argue that minority or female status is now in fact an advantage in pursuing an academic career. Please indicate your beliefs about this issue with regard to the several dimensions of career progress listed below. For each dimension indicate whether minority or female status constitutes a disadvantage (1), an advantage (2), or makes no difference (3).

PROFESSIONAL LIFE-SITUATION VARIABLES

The National Faculty Stress Study contains several variables that can be used to assess the relative job satisfaction of the respondent. Two questions from the "stress" section of the survey are used to determine the respondent's level of satisfaction with the professional life-situation of university employment. The first asks respondents to gauge the level of pressure that they felt from "receiving salary inadequate to meet my needs." The second question asks respondents to assess the level of pressure they felt from "feeling that my career progress is not what it should be."[7] A third job satisfaction variable asks respondents to indicate the extent to which they agree or disagree with the statement: "I feel trapped in a profession with limited opportunities for advancement."[8] A final professional life-situation variable is that of tenure status of the respondent. Tenure is presumed to be held at the associate and full professorial ranks.[9] These variables will be used in the analysis chapter that follows.

NOTES

1. Arthur Biglan's (1973) model divides academic disciplines into eight distinct clusters dealing with hard versus soft paradigms, applied or pure use of knowledge, and life versus nonlife systems.

2. See Walter H. Gmelch, Phyllis Kay Wilke and Nicholas P. Lovrich, "Dimensions of Stress Among University Faculty: Factor-Analytic Results from a National Study," *Reseach in Higher Education.* 24, no. 3 (1986):266-86.

3. Respondents assessed the impact of affirmative action on American universities on the following scale:

Negative Effects Upon Universities				Positive Effects Upon Universities
1	2	3	4	5

4. Respondents assessed the impact of affirmative action on their career and their university on the following scale:

Positive Effect	Some Postive, Some Negative Effects	Negative Effect	Uncertain Effect
1	2	3	4	5

5. Respondents indicated their agreement or disagreement with the reasons against affirmative action on the following scale:

Strongly Disagree		Uncertain		Strongly Agree
1	2	3	4	5

6. The career dimension questions asked respondents to answer within the following format.

Career Dimension

	Disadv.	Advantage	No Difference
Initial Faculty selection	1	2	3

7. Respondents assessed the level of pressure that they felt on the stress questions on the following scale:

No or Slight Pressure		Noticeable Moderate Pressure		High or Excessive Pressure
1	2	3	4	5

8. Respondents indicated the extent to which they agreed or disagreed with feeling trapped in a profession with limited opportunities on the following scale:

Strongly Agree	Agree with Reservations	Disagree with Reservations	Strongly Disagree
1	2	3	4

9. Respondents indicated their Academic rank on the following scale:

___ Instructor/Lecturer
___ Assistant Professor
___ Associate Professor
___ Full Professor

5

Formulating a Model

This section of the study will draw out themes from the reviews of literature presented earlier and suggest ways in which these themes might be tested against the empirical results obtained in the 1986 National Faculty Stress Study.   Through this testing and examination of ideas, greater insight will be gained into perspectives on affirmative action held by university faculty. The major theme to be drawn from the review of literature is that affirmative action can be viewed as a public policy that serves as an excellent focus for the examination of competing--and often incompatible--values in contemporary societies. The conflict inherent in liberal societies between egalitarianism and individualism was outlined (McWilliams 1979), and it was posited that affirmative action provides an excellent opportunity to ask: "Do individuals respond to affirmative action primarily from the ethic of individualism, self-interest, and faith in meritocratic fairness, or do they instead base their views on what they think the public interest requires for the achievement of social equity?"

It will be recalled from Chapter 2 that the liberal political philosophy features an overriding focus on the rights of the individual.   Liberal societies elaborate a multitude of procedural safeguards to ensure that the citizens' autonomy to pursue their self-interest, and rights against government infringements on their liberty are protected to the fullest extent possible. Affirmative action, it was posited, is necessarily problematic in liberal societies because it sometimes requires that equity interests be served by the violation of procedural safeguards for "advantaged" individuals (Dahl 1977);

such procedural safeguards are typically manifested through systems of merit selection and promotion.

Institutions of higher education especially dramatize this problematic nature of affirmative action both because they have been at the forefront of developing voluntary affirmative action programs, and because their professional personnel processes are presumably based on merit. Entrance into the academy as either a student or member of the faculty is structured to reflect intellectual or academic merit. Career progress for faculty is based upon meritocratic achievements in the major areas of teaching, research and service activities. Upward progress through the academic ranks requires achievement in all three areas at most institutions of greater size. The process of upward mobility requires that faculty members pass reviews undertaken by their colleagues, a relatively unique personnel feature of the academic world. The work of each faculty member, in the ideal meritocratic system, is judged on its own merit by one's peers. Those whose work is judged to be of sufficient quality (and quantity) are passed on to the next level, or admitted to the faculty in the first place.

In this meritocratic system, one can assume that an academic's perception of the career progress of an applicant or colleague should reflect this emphasis on the individual. Each scholar should, in the "ideal type" of the university (as might befit Michael Young's (1958) depiction of "meritocracy" in the year 2033), present themselves to their peers for review as individuals, and decisions about that individual should be based on merit. If, however, it is the case that individuals are not perceived as scholars presenting themselves on the basis of their meritocratic achievement, but are instead viewed as members of categorical groups, then we can begin to question the extent to which individuals are taken as individuals. If the system of academic meritocracy were truly intact, then individuals should be indistinguishable from one another on the basis of racial or sexual categories. This color- and gender-neutral nature of the "ideal" academy stems from the primacy of the individual so important in liberal societies, and from the presumed meritocratic system that evaluates individuals on their merit as opposed to their personal characteristics. Academics successfully socialized into the academy would then resemble each other in their belief in the meritocratic nature of academic career progress. However, if it were the case that academics perceived career progress to be based properly on some consideration of categorical information such as race and sex, as opposed to merit exclusively, then the existence of the "ideal" academy could be seriously doubted.

The legitimate pursuit of self-interest was described as a particularly important part of liberal philosophy. The self-interest of academics can be construed as being connected with their professional life-situation, for example, their tenure status or job satisfaction. If academia were in fact a color- and gender neutral meritocracy, these factors would be the only relevant parameters of an academic's career related self-interest. Each individual would be an isolated unit proceeding or failing on the basis of her own meritocratic achievement. If, however, academics perceive their academic career progress to be connected--either to one's advantage or disadvantage--with racial and sexual categories, then this would represent a serious divergence from the belief in the meritocratic academic system.

In that not too uncommon situation, academics would no longer be taken as individuals, but as members of some larger collectivity of either "protected classes" or nonprotected groups. These considerations run counter to liberal ideas about the primacy of the individual and academic traditions calling for career progress to be based exclusively on meritorious achievement. Further, if academics not only perceive academic career progress to be associated with categorical groupings such as race and gender, but academics across all ranks within the profession perceive it in such a way, then truly the primacy of the individual has been lost to a perception of individuals and their value as scholars that is categorical and denies the autonomy of individual scholars and their right to be taken on their own merit. By way of illustration, it may be that untenured white males believe that being a woman or minority scholar is advantageous with regard to important career dimensions. Given the reality of existing affirmative action programs, this would be in line with their career-oriented self-interest in that the perception that women and minorities may be hired and/or promoted preferentially over them is potentially threatening. If, however, not only untenured white males, but tenured and advanced rank white males, for example--who no longer are threatened in their own career progress by women and minority scholars--perceive categorical status to be advantageous, then the divergence from belief in a meritocratic system is quite serious. It would appear in that situation that self-interest as it should manifest itself in an ideal meritocratic academic world--that is, self-interest related to the career position of the individual--is being superceded by the individual's membership in a categorical group--a larger community. These considerations lend some credence to the ideas of writers such as Michael Sandel (1982) and Deborah Stone (1988), who contend that to conceptualize individuals outside of their connections to larger groups and communities is fundamentally inappropriate. Sandel points to this as a major flaw of liberalism as it is developed by writers such as Rawls. Individuals do not, in the end, exist in splendid isolation but rather as members of groups and communities of meaning which contribute to their world view beyond mere self-interest. This study will ask: Do university faculty perceive career progress to reflect such community connections as those based upon the categorical groupings of race and sex, and is their perception of this state of affairs related to the academic's own racial and gender status?

A first step in assessing whether university faculty do respond to the policy of affirmative action according to these categorical groupings is to attempt to determine whether significant differences exist in attitudes based on racial and sexual categories. The use of the matched-pairs sample (matched by race--black to white--and by gender--male to male/female to female, tenure status, age, type of university, discipline and marital status) allows us to examine differences in the perceptions of male and female and minority and non-minority faculty with many simultaneous controls for relevant background factors. That is, the many controls provided by the matched-pairs sample allows one to suggest with greater certainty that differences between whites and blacks or men and women are due to their race or sex and not to some other difference, such as tenure status or discipline, which may be related to gender and/or race. Since women and minority faculty in the aggregate are decidedly junior in rank, more likely to be untenured, unmarried and in the soft science or humanities disciplines, direct comparisons of aggregates are terribly misleading. Such aggregate comparisons often lead to incorrect attributions of gender and race differences (Rice and Jones 1984). The paired t-test for comparison of means will be employed to examine the differences in black and white faculty perceptions of affirmative action. If significant differences are found in the responses of black and white, male and female faculty regarding these issues, then it can be assumed that important differences do in fact exist among faculty based on their categorical status.

The extent to which meritocracy is believed to be compromised by affirmative action can be assessed by the National Faculty Stress study in several ways. First, a set of questions is available in which respondents expressed their view as to whether it is an advantage, a disadvantage or whether it makes no difference to be a minority or woman with regard to fifteen individual career dimensions relevant to academic career progress--such as initial faculty selection, salary, promotions and tenure review. This set of questions will be used to assess respondents' belief in the meritocratic nature of academia. If academic progress is based on merit alone, then certainly it would make no difference to be either a woman or a minority with regard to the mentioned career dimensions. The extent to which meritocracy may be perceived to be compromised by racial or sexual status can be gauged by examining the advantage response. That is, do respondents believe that it is an advantage to be either a female or minority with regard to important career dimensions? Meritocracy may be perceived to be compromised in the opposite way as well, that is, in terms of it being a disadvantage to be a minority or woman scholar with regard to career dimensions important to academic progress. Perceptions of disadvantages associated with racial and sexual categories also represent a departure from progress based purely on the basis of merit.

In keeping with the idea that an ideal meritocratic academia would structure career progress only on the basis of merit, and that the legitimate pursuit of self-interest within that environment would be related to professional life-situation conditions such as seeking success in an imminent tenure review, the National Faculty Stress Study allows one to examine the extent to which relevant factors about respondents--tenure status, academic rank or measures of job satisfaction--are associated with their perceptions of affirmative action and the relative advantage or disadvantage of being a minority or woman scholar. It is assumed that only those individuals facing threatening career situations--namely, untenured faculty members or those dissatisfied with their career choice or outlook--will consider minority or female status an advantage (or disadvantage) with regard to important career dimensions. If scholars who have reached the career security of tenure and advanced rank, and/or are satisfied with their career progress, perceive minority or female status to be an advantage (or disadvantage) with regard to important career dimensions, then one can assume that these faculty are reacting to other scholars and perceiving this policy issue in terms of categorical groupings as opposed to individual achievement. This would suggest that the micro-level resolution of the conflicting values inherent in affirmative action (those of the self-interest of the individual versus the need to sometimes violate procedual safeguards of individual rights for the sake of greater equity) is one of perceiving the policy in categorical terms as opposed to self-interest terms--at least in the somewhat narrowly conceived form of self interest described here as part of the meritocratic ideal academia. These questions can be addressed through the use of cross-tabulations of these life-situation variables by the perceived advantage, disadvantage or no difference accruing to minority and women scholars with regard to important career dimensions.

By using the demographic and professional life-situation information from the survey (for example, race, gender and tenure status), we can posit a "self-interest" position for each respondent with regard to affirmative action policy. We can assume, for example, that white males facing an imminent tenure review or considering leaving their current academic position would find affirmative action policies to be a threat to their self-interest. It is also reasonable to assume that white males who have little or no productivity in publishing may feel the most threatened by women and minorities.

Preferential hiring and promotion of women and minorities may result in the delay or denial of the white male's promotion or hiring. If white males facing this critical career turning point respond to affirmative action out of "self-interest," then we should find that they evaluate affirmative action more negatively in general in its impact on the university, in the belief that affirmative action has had negative effects on their own career, and that affirmative action makes it an advantage to be a woman or minority scholar with regard to important career dimensions. These questions can be examined through the use of descriptive statistics such as cross-tabulation tables, or the use of paired t-tests to compare with black scholars as described later.

The framework for determining whether or not self-interest influences minority and woman scholars' attitudes toward affirmative action is not the same as it is for white males. As noted in Chapter 2, affirmative action may serve to "devalue" the achievements of women and minorities and perpetuate the idea that these groups cannot achieve without preferential help. If women and minority scholars perceive that affirmative action "perpetuates the myth of minority and female inferiority" and/or that affirmative action programs "rob minorities and women of a clear sense of deserved accomplishment," then we can expect their self-interest to dictate a perception that affirmative action programs have negative impacts in general, and negative impacts on their own career specifically. These questions can be examined through the use of descriptive statistics such as cross tabulation tables.

Women and minority scholars who do not perceive that affirmative action programs perpetuate myths of female and minority inferiority may indeed perceive affirmative action programs to be in their self-interest. We should expect that these individuals will perceive that affirmative action programs have had positive effects in general and on their own careers, and that it is an advantage to be a woman or minority scholar with regard to important career dimensions. Once again, these factors can be examined through the use of descriptive statistics such as cross-tabulation tables.

A second theme developed in Chapter 2 is that other studies of attitudes toward affirmative action and issues of racial equity tend to suggest that support for these issues is high in the abstract, but considerably lower when specific implementations of affirmative action are faced by respondents. It was suggested in that discussion that affirmative action represents a conflict between values involving the maintenance of the primacy of the individual and that individual's legitimate pursuit of self-interest, and the need to control or determine the final distribution of goods in society so that that distribution is in the end more equitable (Carens 1981:1-22). In examining previous studies of attitudes about affirmative action, it seems that Americans tend to resolve this conflict by supporting the abstract idea of equality and the notion of affirmative action in the general sense, but express resistance to specific steps to achieve that equality or to implement affirmative action when the value of individualism and individual achievement is too directly challenged (Kariel 1977:18-33). Do participants in the National Faculty Stress Study respond to questions about affirmative action in the same way as participants in these other studies reviewed earlier? Can we expect that our most educated professionals, embedded in a meritocratic system, will reflect the same pattern in their attitudes about affirmative action as the general population? These questions can be examined by looking at the respondents to the National Faculty Stress Study's answers to questions that address the impact of affirmative action on universities in general versus its impact on their own career or their own university. A cross-tabulation across these two types of variables will demonstrate the extent to which support for affirmative action among faculty is limited to the general as opposed to the specific, thereby resembling or differing from the attitudinal patterns of the general public.

Another specific idea that was presented in the literature review is the notion that people attribute less qualification to women and minorities because of affirmative action programs--a tendency, to the extent that it persists--which serves to perpetuate myths of their inferiority (Glazer 1975). It was discussed that the greater the deviation from "merit," the greater the resistance to the policy. The entrance of women and minorities into the work force in greater numbers, some of which employment is due directly to the impact of affirmative action policies, may associate the hiring and promotion of all women and minorities, in the eyes of white males, with a system of highly preferential treatment that compromises merit. The true merit of women and minority scholars may be obscured, according to this line of reasoning, by the assumption that they were hired or promoted only as a result of affirmative action policies and not on the weight of their own merit. This question can be examined by looking at the responses to the two questions dealing with contending perceptions of affirmative action. Do respondents express a belief in these assertions that affirmative action perpetuates the myth of minority and female inferiority? Once again, relevant demographic and career factors such as race, gender, tenure status, job satisfaction and productivity can be used to determine if only particular groups lend credence to these beliefs about affirmative action.

6

Analysis of Data

This chapter will draw out themes from the review of literature, state those themes in terms of testable propositions, and then test these propositions against the empirical results obtained from the 1986 National Faculty Stress Study. A description of how the research questions to be tested here were derived from the conceptual chapter is contained in the preceding chapter.

GENERAL AND SPECIFIC ATTITUDES TOWARD AFFIRMATIVE ACTION

A major theme addressed throughout this study is the relative importance of self-interest and a general concern for equitable public policy in the perception and evaluation of affirmative action policies. In order to assess the extent to which the presumed self-interest of university faculty is reflected in attitudes about affirmative action, each of the categorical groupings of faculty (white men, white women, black men and black women) can be arrayed along a continuum of perceived threat from affirmative action and their respective levels of support for affirmative action can be compared (see Figure 6.1). If self-interest--as reflected in the perception of affirmative action as a threat--is an overriding factor in determining support for affirmative action, both in general abstract terms and in specific concrete outcomes, then one should expect to find levels of support that affirmative action has had a positive impact on their own career is much greater than their general abstract support for the policy (83

Figure 6.1
Graphical Presentation of Attitudes Toward Affirmative Action

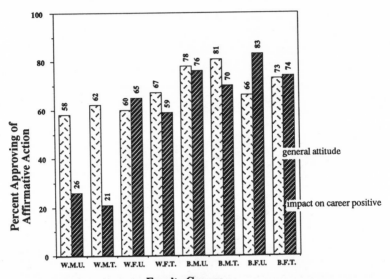

Faculty Groups
Order of groups: White males untenured, tenured; White females
untenured, tenured; Black males untenured,
tenured; Black females untenured, tenured.

percent for the former as opposed to 66 percent for the latter). Many
of the black female faculty who supplied open-ended comments on
the survey noted that intial advantages accrued to them because of
their race and gender, but that that intial advantage disappeared in
the face of continued racism and sexism on campus. One black female
assistant professor writes, "My gender and race have helped me get
noticed by departments, but once in, these same attributes have been
as big a liability as they always were. Racism and sexism are still
alive and well in most university departments."

The trends implied in these data (see Figure 6.2) indicate clearly
that, as the presumption of the primacy of self-interest would dictate, the perception that affirmative action has had a positive impact
on one's own career increases monotonically as one progresses along

Figure 6.2
A Linear Presentation of Attitudes Toward Affirmative Action

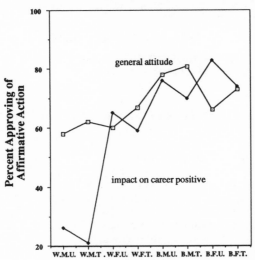

Faculty Groups
Order of groups: White males untenured, tenured; White females
untenured, tenured; Black males untenured,
tenured; Black females untenured, tenured.

the continuum of tenured and untenured academic groups according
to the expected perceived threat from affirmative action to each group.
The trend for general support for affirmative action is similar: that
is, support for affirmative action as a public policy increases as the
threat to self-interest decreases. The magnitude of the difference in
support for the general impact of the policy along the continuum is
smaller--ranging across 23 percentage points--as compared to a range
of 62 points for the trend line representing perceptions of the positive impact on one's own career. In sum, then, trends in attitudes
toward affirmative action that are both general in regard to impacts
on universities and specific in regard to impacts on one's own career
clearly reflect the hypothesized primacy of self-interest calculations
on the part of the faculty respondents. As the threat to one's self-
interest from affirmative action increases, support for the policy in

both general and specific terms decreases. Conversely, as the potential disadvantage to one's self-interest from affirmative action decreases, support for the policy in both general and specific terms increases.

CATEGORICAL GROUP DIFFERENCES IN ATTITUDES TOWARD AFFIRMATIVE ACTION

Difference of Means Tests for Matched Pairs of University Faculty

The next dimension of findings to be addressed is whether or not significant differences in the perceptions of white and black academics are in evidence. If a meritocratic system actually obtains within academia, then academics should differ little from one another on the basis of gender or race in questions of personnel practices--that is, selection, promotion and tenure, gaining support for research and so on. In order to assess whether gender and race differences exist, difference of means tests were conducted on the responses of matched pairs of black and white academics to the set of questions assessing the impact of affirmative action on the career dimensions of minority and women scholars. These results are reported in Table 6.1, and these findings suggest significant differences between the responses of whites and blacks with regard to several important career dimensions. There are statistically significant differences between black and white assessments of the impact of affirmative action on the career prospects of the intended beneficiaries of affirmative action for each of the fifteen career dimensions in relation to minority scholars, with white academics assessing minority status as a much greater advantage than black academics perceive. It should be recalled that these differences appear in spite of the fact that the matched-pair t-test controls for the effects of tenure status, academic discipline, type of institution, age and marital status. This matched-pair t-test statistical procedure allows the analyst to suggest with considerable certainty that the differences in evidence are due to the difference in race as opposed to some other factor that might create this divergence in perception (Blalock 1979:236-37).

It appears from Table 6.1 that differences in the perception of white and black faculty with regard to the impacts of affirmative action on the careers of women scholars are somewhat less marked than is the case for minority academics. In only three dimensions--graduate course assignments, clerical support and professional interaction with colleagues--average responses as to whether minority status is an advantage, makes no difference, or is a disadvantage

Table 6.1
Difference of Means Tests for Matched Pairs of University Faculty for the Impact of Affirmative Action on the Career Dimensions of Minority and Female Scholars

Career Dimension	Impact on Minority Scholars Mean Scores			Impact on Women Scholars Mean Scores		
	White	Black	T-Value	White	Black	T-Value
Initial faculty selection	2.71	1.95	9.93***	2.49	2.31	2.15*
Undergraduate course assignments	1.96	1.76	4.27***	1.96	1.83	2.28*
Graduate course assignments	1.92	1.57	6.65***	1.87	1.75	1.79
Salary consideration	2.26	1.67	8.66***	1.75	1.61	1.99*
Tenure review	2.40	1.45	14.05***	2.12	1.61	6.67***
Ability to obtain grants and publications	2.22	1.52	11.07***	2.09	1.81	3.81***
Promotion in rank	2.24	1.42	13.83***	1.93	1.67	3.46***
Assignment of advising duties	1.88	1.57	5.42***	1.87	1.74	2.16*
Committee assignments	1.87	1.56	4.82***	1.86	1.71	2.05*
Administrative assignments	2.01	1.49	7.38***	1.93	1.58	4.78***
Clerical support	1.93	1.69	5.34***	1.84	1.81	0.69
Mentoring by senior colleagues	1.78	1.33	8.06***	1.78	1.63	2.00*
Professional interaction with colleagues	1.68	1.31	6.91***	1.69	1.62	1.10
Social interaction with colleagues	1.60	1.55	4.94***	1.87	1.75	2.08*
Interdepartmental communication	1.82	1.55	4.94***	1.87	1.75	2.08*

* Indicates $p < 0.05$.
** Indicates $p < 0.01$.
*** Indicates $p < 0.001$.

among whites and blacks are not statistically significant. In all but four of the significantly different perceptions of affirmative action impacts on career dimensions for women scholars, the degree to which whites and blacks differ is smaller in regard to impacts on women scholars than for impacts on minority scholars. White academics, more so than their black counterparts, tend to see protected category status as having more of an advantage for minority scholars than for women scholars in regard to important career dimensions. The divergence between the races is larger with regard to impact on the careers of minority scholars than on the careers of women scholars, even though being a minority or female scholar is considered an advantage for both groups of scholars. In sum, it appears from Table 6.1 that the proposed "ideal" academic meritocratic situation--that is, one in which individuals are not distinguishable on the basis of categorical groupings--does not hold for this sample of university faculty.

Principal Components Factor Analysis

To further assess the extent to which this sample of university faculty may or may not differ on the basis of their categorical groupings, a factor analysis was conducted on the fifteen career dimensions for which the respondents indicated whether it was a disadvantage, an advantage, or makes no difference to be a minority or woman scholar. If university faculty are indistinguishable on the basis of racial categorical groupings, then the various career dimension indicators should load similarly for whites and blacks on the various factors or dimensions that emerge from these data. Tables 6.2 and 6.3 report the results of principal components (varimax rotated) factor analysis for white and black faculty, respectively.

Nine dimensions emerged in the responses of the white faculty, while the analysis of the responses of the black faculty produced ten dimensions. There are important differences in the way in which responses on these career dimensions load on the factors that emerge for the two faculty groups. The career dimension variables with the highest loading on the factor that explains the greatest percentage of the variance differs substantially for the two groups of faculty. A factor highlighting interpersonal communication variables is most prominent for white faculty (eigenvalue = 8.8, 29.3 percent of the variance explained); in contrast, career dimensions related to pay and promotional considerations--such as tenure review, salary consideration and promotion, have the highest loadings on the most prominent factor for black faculty (eigenvalue = 7.31, 24.4 percent of the variance explained).

Table 6.2
Principal Components (varimax rotated) Factor Matrix of the Career Dimension Items for White Respondents

Career Dimension	Factors								
	1	2	3	4	5	6	7	8	9
Professional interaction with colleagues--minority	**.67**	.13	.03	.16	.12	.17	-.05	.08	.16
Professional interaction with colleagues--woman	**.75**	.06	.07	.19	.08	.20	.03	.13	.08
Social interaction with colleagues--minority	**.77**	.04	.13	.08	.18	-.11	.00	-.10	.15
Social interaction with colleagues--woman	**.70**	.03	.09	.01	.21	.12	.13	-.03	.18
Initial faculty selection--minority	.25	**.46**	.06	.14	.06	.34	.22	.34	.15
Initial faculty selection--woman	.20	**.72**	.08	-.16	-.16	.15	.04	.14	-.22
Salary consideration--woman	.22	**.62**	.09	.01	.25	-.21	.09	.02	.33
Tenure review--minority	-.07	**.56**	.23	.38	.25	.23	-.02	.04	.18
Tenure review--woman	.02	**.78**	.12	.23	.11	.07	.11	.02	.09
Promotion in rank--minority	-.16	**.47**	.24	.32	.26	**.42**	-.10	-.01	.10

Table 6.2 (Continued)

Career Dimension	1	2	3	4	5	6	7	8	9
Promotion in rank--woman	.05	**.79**	.10	.14	.12	.08	.12	.06	.20
Assignment of advising Duties--woman	.19	.14	**.48**	.03	**.46**	.03	**.44**	.17	.10
Committee assignments--minority	.01	.04	**.83**	.04	.17	.17	.02	.11	.01
Graduate course assignments--minority	.26	.17	.05	**.84**	.09	-.02	.25	.05	-.01
Graduate course assignments--woman	.28	.17	.10	**.77**	.06	-.11	.23	.18	.11
Mentoring by senior colleagues--minority	.35	.20	.05	.10	**.73**	.00	.00	.22	.04
Mentoring by senior colleagues--woman	**.46**	.09	.06	.17	**.72**	.05	.08	.13	.02
Assignment of advising duties--minority	.11	.14	**.46**	.00	**.51**	.21	.38	.17	.03
Ability to obtain grants and publications--minority	.17	.03	.11	.01	.13	**.86**	.08	.10	.10
Ability to obtain grants and publications--woman	.26	.34	.15	-.17	-.16	**.66**	.17	.05	.10
Undergraduate course assignments--minority	.05	.05	.07	**.42**	.21	.22	**.71**	.00	-.01

Factors

	Factor 1	Factor 2	Factor 3	Factor 4	Factor 5	Factor 6	Factor 7	Factor 8	Factor 9
Undergraduate course assignments--woman	-.01	.12	.24	.16	-.03	-.01	**.74**	.20	.14
Clerical support--minority	-.03	.02	.26	.14	.19	.19	.09	**.80**	.08
Clerical support--woman	.07	.16	.20	.06	.14	-.03	.16	**.87**	.08
Interdepartmental communication--minority	**.44**	.10	-.02	-.03	-.04	.01	.04	.08	**.73**
Salary consideration--minority	-.02	.15	.25	.36	.27	.14	-.26	.07	**.52**
Interdepartmental communication--woman	.32	.14	-.10	.05	.00	.15	.23	.10	**.77**

Factor	Eigenvalue	Percent of Variance
One	8.78805	29.3
Two	2.73547	9.1
Three	2.20115	7.3
Four	1.86011	6.2
Five	1.45273	4.8
Six	1.34573	4.5
Seven	1.24209	4.1
Eight	1.15447	3.8
Nine	1.06025	3.5

Note: The boldface numbers highlight the highest loading items on each of the factors.
Total variance = 72.6%.

Table 6.3
Principal Components (varimax rotated) Factor Matrix of the Career Dimension Items for Black Respondents

Career Dimension	Factors									
	1	2	3	4	5	6	7	8	9	10
Salary consideration--minority	.67	-.03	-.17	-.02	.19	.27	.26	-.05	-.02	.19
Salary consideration--woman	.73	.14	.21	-.15	.18	.17	.13	-.15	-.05	.12
Tenure review--minority	.67	-.09	-.14	.41	.06	.17	.05	.22	.11	.07
Tenure review--woman	.78	-.05	-.36	.05	.16	.00	-.04	.16	.08	-.08
Promotion in rank--minority	.68	-.02	-.13	.46	-.03	.13	.04	.10	.24	.14
Promotion in rank--woman	.71	.07	.31	.02	.04	.03	.02	.10	.35	-.08
Assignment of advising duties--minority	.01	.81	-.04	.17	.01	-.02	.21	.07	-.17	.06
Assignment of advising duties--woman	-.05	.79	.09	.08	.12	.03	.35	.02	.02	.00
Committee assignment--minority	.01	.74	.11	.15	.21	.00	-.22	.24	-.03	.09
Committee assignments--woman	.04	.83	.09	-.05	.10	.01	.01	.21	.13	.04
Professional interaction with colleagues--woman	.16	.03	.73	.14	.10	-.03	.22	.12	.20	.04
Social interaction with colleagues--woman	.07	.10	.85	.21	.11	.04	.02	.10	-.05	.10

Interdepartmental communication--woman	.06	.14	**.60**	.23	.15	.23	.44	.17	.31	-.10
Professional interaction with colleagues--minority	.14	.12	.14	**.76**	.13	-.15	.10	.03	.09	.09
Social interaction with colleagues--minorities	.02	.20	.33	**.69**	.01	-.06	-.15	.03	-.23	.12
Interdepartmental communication--minorities	-.01	.08	.14	**.65**	.10	.17	.37	.12	.23	-.06
Undergraduate course assignments--minority	.11	.22	-.08	.25	**.72**	.28	.03	-.02	.16	.00
Undergraduate course assignments--woman	.10	.34	.18	-.06	**.74**	.14	.02	-.14	.17	-.02
Graduate course assignments--minority	.12	-.15	-.02	.30	**.71**	.04	.13	.24	-.03	.19
Graduate course assignments--woman	.18	.14	.34	-.11	**.74**	-.05	.09	.13	-.01	.02
Initial faculty selection--minority	.20	-.06	-.09	.07	.13	**.88**	.03	.07	-.07	-.01
Initial faculty selection--woman	.20	.07	.19	-.13	.10	**.82**	-.06	.03	.11	-.03
Clerical support--minority	.15	.07	.04	.28	.19	.02	**.74**	.08	-.15	.07
Clerical support--woman	.11	.21	.26	-.10	-.02	-.10	**.70**	.12	.08	.09
Assignment of administrative tasks--minority	.03	.39	.05	.13	.08	.03	.03	**.80**	-.08	.06
Assignment of administrative tasks--woman	.15	.18	.22	.04	.05	.08	.22	**.82**	.08	.01

Table 6.3 (Continued)

Career Dimension	Factors									
	1	2	3	4	5	6	7	8	9	10
Ability to obtain grants and publication--minority	.11	.02	-.05	.39	.23	.19	.04	.04	**.63**	.24
Ability to obtain grants and publications--woman	.35	-.09	.27	-.08	.07	-.11	-.05	-.05	**.72**	.06
Mentoring by senior colleagues--minority	.12	.13	-.08	.34	.06	-.13	.01	.04	.11	**.80**
Mentoring by senior colleagues--woman	.09	.09	.49	-.18	.10	.13	.20	.04	.09	**.71**

Factor	Eigenvalue	Percent of Variance
One	7.30943	24.4
Two	3.40204	11.0
Three	2.28266	7.6
Four	2.15229	7.2
Five	1.67721	5.6
Six	1.49189	5.0
Seven	1.35896	4.5
Eight	1.13877	3.8
Nine	1.08327	3.6
Ten	1.04115	3.5

Notes: The highlighted numbers are the highest loading items in each factor. Total variance = 76.2.

Further differences are found in the way some specific career dimension indicators load on separate factors for the two faculty groups. For minority faculty, for example, initial faculty selection and mentoring by senior colleagues each load on separate factors; for white faculty, however, these career dimension variables are intermixed with other career dimensions. It is also interesting to note that for black faculty, the measures of the impact of minority or female status on social and professional interaction with colleagues and interdepartmental communication load on separate factors when the impact is being assessed for minority as opposed to female scholars. For white faculty respondents, these variables load on a single factor, which is also the most prominent factor for the responses of that group.

In sum, the pattern of findings evident in the tandem factor analyses for white and black faculty for fifteen career dimensions related to academic career progress is that of noteworthy racial differences. These results, in combination with the findings from the difference of means tests--indicating clearly that significant interracial differences in perception obtain--lead to the conclusion that the ideal academy in which "color-blind" justice among faculty serves to make racial classifications irrelevant in faculty perceptions of personnel practices does not exist as a general rule.

THE IMPACT OF PROFESSIONAL LIFE-SITUATION VARIABLES ON ATTITUDES TOWARD AFFIRMATIVE ACTION

In Chapter 5 it was argued that in the ideal academy, faculty members are taken as individuals whose status and standing is determined exclusively on the basis of their merit. In such circumstances, it would follow that certain important aspects of one's job situation, such as the degree of job satisfaction or the proximity of a tenure review decision, should be far more compelling influences on faculty attitudes about academic career progress than racial or gender traits. In order to assess the relative effects of these professional-life situation variables and race and gender characteristics with respect to attitudes about career progress, measures of these several variables were cross-tabulated. Four specific career progress variables were selected for analysis: initial faculty selection, tenure review, salary consideration and mentoring by senior colleagues. These variables were cross-tabulated with the following attitudinal measures of professional life situation: "feeling as if my career progress is not what it should be," "feeling trapped in a profession with limited opportunities," and "receiving inadequate salary to meet my needs." The additional important "objective-circumstance" profes-

Table 6.4

Relationships between Measures of Affirmative Action Impact on Selected Career Dimensions and the Tenure Status of Respondents

Career Dimension	White Male	White Female	Black Male	Black Female
Initial faculty selection--minority	.06	.01	-.20	.10
Initial faculty selection--woman	-.20	.08	-.11	.10
Tenure review--minority	.14	.20	.15	.33
Tenure Review--woman	.10	.14	.40	.53
Salary consideration--minority	.03	-.17	.23	.30
Salary consideration--woman	.24	.34	.30	.42
Mentoring by senior colleagues--minority	.44	.00	.25	-.14
Mentoring by senior colleagues--woman	.39	.13	-.02	.04

Note: The tenure status measure was constructed from the academic rank of the respondents. Associate and full professors were assumed to have tenure, while lecturers and assistant professors were assumed not to have tenure.

sional life-situation variable of tenured/nontenured status of the respondent was also cross-tabulated with the four career progress dimensions. The gamma statistic, which is appropriate for estimating degree of association for ordinal or ranked data, is reported for the associations found between measures of minority or female status on selected career dimensions--initial faculty selection, tenure review, salary consideration and mentoring--and the four measures of professional life situation in Tables 6.4 through 6.7. No significance testing was conducted on the gamma statistics. In keeping with conventional practice, a level at which gamma statistics are considered noteworthy was selected (see, for example, Hawkins et al. 1986). For the purposes of this study, gammas larger than 0.20 (or -0.20) will be discussed as 'noteworthy.'

Relationships between Tenure Status of Respondent and Perception of Impact of Minority or Female Status on Career Dimensions

Table 6.4 reports gammas from cross-tabulations of the minority or female status impacts on career progress variables and the respondent's tenure/non-tenure status for white males, white females, black males and black females. The results displayed in Table 6.4 reveal that several of the career dimension/tenure status cross-tabulations produce noteworthy gammas. Positive gamma statistics indicate that tenured faculty respondents tend to perceive that it is an advantage to be a minority or woman scholar with regard to the career progress dimensions or that untenured faculty perceive that protected group status is a disadvantage. Negative gamma statistics indicate that tenured faculty respondents tend to preceive that it is a disadvantage to be a minority or woman scholar with regard to the career progress dimensions, and that untenured faculty consider that it is an advantage.

Among black women respondents, the salary consideration for women's career dimension is positively related to tenure status (gamma =0.42); 78.8 percent of the untenured black female faculty express the opinion that it is a disadvantage to be a woman with regard to salary consideration. Regardless of tenure status in fact, 63.6 percent of the black female faculty respondents opine that it is a disadvantage to be a women scholar with regard to salary considerations as compared to 26.0 percent who feel that it makes no difference and only 10.4 percent who believe that it is an advantage. These figures should be contrasted to the responses from white males who, across tenure status categories, produced the following results: 55.6 percent felt that it made no difference to be a woman with regard to salary consideration, and 21.8 percent and 22.6 percent believed that it was a disadvantage and an advantage, respectively.

The strength of the relationships between tenure status and the selected career dimension measures is very different across the four categories of academics. For example, there are noteworthy relationships between "tenure review women" and tenure status for both black males and black females (gammas of 0.40 and 0.53, respectively), while neither of the relationships between these variables is noteworthy for white males and white females. This suggests that the relationship between tenure status and the impact of tenure review on minorities is stronger for black respondents than for white respondents. The same pattern is found in the cross-tabulation of the impact of salary consideration for minority scholars and tenure status. Here again the relationships between these variables are stronger for black respondents than for whites, with gammas of 0.23 for black male respondents and 0.30 for black female faculty.

In sum, the professional life-situation variable of tenure status is related to the perception that being a minority or woman scholar is an advantage or disadvantage on important career dimensions in fifteen out of thirty-two cross-tabulations reported in Table 6.4. In only one instance--that of the impact of being a woman on salary consideration--is there a noteworthy relationship between tenure status and the career dimension for all racial and gender categorical groups. However, these relationships vary in strength: the gamma for white males is 0.24 while the gamma for black females is 0.42, indicating that the relationship between tenure status and salary consideration for women is stronger for black women than for white males. These findings add further evidence to support the conclusion that categorical group membership is more important to understanding perceptions of how protected group status affects career progress than is the important job-situation variable of tenure status.

Relationship between Job Satisfaction Variables and the Perception of Impact of Minority or Female Status on Career Dimensions

Table 6.5 reports gammas for the cross-tabulations of the minority or female status impacts on career progress variables and the job satisfaction variable "feeling pressure from receiving an inadequate salary to meet my needs." Only one of the career dimension/ inadequate salary cross-tabulations for black men (salary consideration for women, gamma = 0.31), and two of the cross-tabulations for white men result in noteworthy gammas (initial faculty selection--minority, gamma = -0.32; and initial faculty selection--women, gamma = -0.22). Four of the eight career dimension/inadequate salary cross-tabulations--initial faculty selection--women (gamma = 0.24), tenure review--women (gamma = -0.25), salary consideration--women (gamma = -0.25) and mentoring by senior colleagues--women (gamma = -0.30)--have noteworthy gammas for white women. Four of the career dimension cross-tabulations were also noteworthy for black women: initial faculty selection--minority (gamma = 0.27), tenure review--minority (gamma = 0.20), salary

Table 6.5

**Relationships between Measures of Affirmative Action Impact
on Selected Career Dimensions and the Job Satisfaction
Variable "Feeling Pressure from Receiving an Inadequate
Salary to Meet One's Needs"**

Career Dimension	White Male	White Female	Black Male	Black Female
Initial faculty selection--minority	-.32	.17	-.07	.27
Initial faculty selection--woman	-.22	.24	-.06	-.14
Tenure review--minority	-.01	-.03	-.06	.20
Tenure review--woman	.05	-.25	-.13	.00
Salary consideration--minority	.05	.13	-.15	-.29
Salary consideration--woman	.02	-.25	-.31	-.28
Mentoring by senior colleagues--minority	-.10	-.11	-.14	.17
Mentoring by senior colleagues--woman	.03	-.30	-.08	.18

Note: Respondents assessed the level of pressure that they felt about salary on the following scale:

No or slight Pressure		Moderate Pressure		Excessive Pressure
1	2	3	4	5

consideration--minority (gamma = -0.29) and salary consideration--women (gamma = -0.28). Once again, many of the gammas are negative, indicating an inverse relationship. To illustrate, the -0.32 gamma for white males on the cross-tabulation of the inadequate salary variable with initial faculty selection of minorities variable indicates that as white males feel lower pressure from receiving an "inadequate salary to meet their needs," their perception that it is an advantage to be a minority with regard to initial faculty selection increases. This is reflected in the actual cross-tabulation, in which 48 percent of the white males' responses fall in the cell "low pressure from receiving an inadequate salary" and "advantage" to be a minority with regard to initial faculty selection.

Although on the surface it might be expected that there would be a strong relationship between feeling pressure about receiving an inadequate salary to meet one's needs and salary consideration for minority scholars, only one of the cross-tabulations results in a noteworthy gamma--that of -0.29 for black women respondents. The inverse relationship indicates that as the perceived pressure from receiving an inadequate salary increases for black women, the perception that it is a disadvantage to be a minority scholar increases. Differently stated, as the perceived pressure from receiving an inadequate salary decreases, the perception that it is an advantage to be a minority scholar increases. In fact, 35 percent of black women respondents fall into the cell which indicates high pressure from receiving an inadequate salary to meet one's needs and the perception that it is a disadvantage to be a minority scholar with regard to salary consideration. The cross-tabulations of the variable salary consideration for women with the career dimension variables, however, results in noteworthy gammas for white women, black men and black women (gammas = -0.25, -0.31 and -0.28, respectively). Each of these noteworthy gammas is negative, indicating, as noted above, that as the pressure from receiving an inadequate salary increases, the perception that it is a disadvantage to be a woman in regard to salary consideration increases; or, conversely, as pressure from receiving an inadequate salary decreases, the perception that it is an advantage to be a woman increases.

In sum, only one-third of the cross-tabulations reported in Table 6.5 result in noteworthy gammas, indicating that the job satisfaction variable of "feeling pressure from receiving an inadequate salary to meet one's needs" is not strongly related to the perceived advantage or disadvantage of being a minority or woman scholar with regard to important career progress dimensions. The pattern of the relationships across the categorical groups is not consistent either in strength or direction, indicating once again that race and sex may account for variations in the distributions of responses to a greater extent than job satisfaction as defined in terms of feeling pressure from receiving an inadequate salary.

Table 6.6 reports gammas from cross-tabulations of the minority or female status impact on career progress variables and the job satisfaction variable "feeling trapped in a profession with limited opportunities." The most striking of the noteworthy gammas result-

Table 6.6
Relationships between Measures of Affirmative Action Impact on Selected Career Dimensions and the Job Satisfaction Variable "Feeling Trapped in a Profession with Limited Opportunity"

Career Dimension	White Male	White Female	Black Male	Black Female
Initial faculty selection--minority	.25	-.33	.00	-.27
Initial faculty selection--woman	.10	-.27	-.22	-.30
Tenure review--minority	-.10	.27	.26	.04
Tenure review--woman	.03	.19	.10	-.30
Salary consideration--minority	-.13	.04	-.01	.05
Salary consideration--woman	-.17	.24	.00	-.10
Mentoring by senior colleagues--minority	.10	.21	.25	-.29
Mentoring by senior colleagues--woman	.02	-.01	-.01	-.51

Note: Respondents indicated the extent to which they agreed or disagreed with feeling trapped in a profession with limited opportunities on the following scale:

Strongly Agree	Agree With Reservations	Disagree with Reservations	Strongly Disagree
1	2	3	4

ing from this series of crosstabulations is that of -0.51 for black women respondents on the cross-tabulation of the impact of mentoring by senior colleagues for faculty women with the variable "feeling trapped in a profession with limited opportunity." The inverse relationship indicates that as the extent to which respondents disagree with the statement that they feel trapped in a profession with limited opportunities increases, the perception that it is a disadvantage to be a woman with regard to mentoring by senior colleagues increases. In fact, 37.5 percent of all the black women respondents fell into the cell "disagreement with feeling trapped in a profession with limited opportunity" and the perception that it is a disadvantage to be a women scholar with regard to mentoring by senior colleagues. None of the other cross-tabulations of mentoring by senior colleagues with feeling trapped in a profession with limited opportunity for the other categorical groups resulted in noteworthy gammas.

Another interesting series of results is found among the cross-tabulations of initial faculty selection for minorities with feeling trapped in a profession with limited opportunity. This cross-tabulation for white males produces a positive noteworthy gamma of 0.25, indicating that as disagreement with the statement of feeling trapped in a profession with limited opportunity increases, the perception that it is an advantage to be a minority with regard to initial faculty selection increases; conversely, as agreement with the statement of feeling trapped in a profession with limited opportunity increases, the perception that it is a disadvantage to be a minority with regard to initial faculty selection increases. It should be noted that, indeed, 60 percent of white male respondents fall into the cell "disagree with feeling trapped in a profession with limited opportunities" and perceive that it is an advantage to be a minority with regard to initial faculty selection. The vast majority (81 percent) of white males, however, perceive it to be an advantage to be a minority with regard to initial faculty selection.

In sharp contrast, the cross-tabulation of initial faculty selection for minorities and "feeling trapped in a profession with limited opportunity" for both white females and black females, however, produces negative noteworthy gammas. Black women, for example, have a negative gamma of -0.27 for this cross-tabulation, indicating that as disagreement with the feeling of being trapped in a profession with limited opportunity increases, the perception that it is a disadvantage to be a minority with regard to initial faculty selection increases; stated conversely, as agreement with the feeling of being trapped in a profession with limited opportunity increases, the perception that it is an advantage to be a minority with regard to initial faculty selection increases.

Another set of gammas in which there is disagreement across categorical groups in terms of the direction of the relationship involves mentoring by senior colleagues for minorities. In this case, both white females and black males have positive noteworthy gamma statistics (gamma = 0.21 and 0.25, respectively), while for black women the relationship is inverted, producing a negative gamma of -0.29.

Table 6.7
Relationships between Measures of Affirmative Action Impact on Selected Career Dimensions and the Job Satisfaction Variable "Feeling that Career Progress Is Not What It Should Be"

Career Dimension	White Male	White Female	Black Male	Black Female
Initial faculty selection--minority	.00	.00	-.07	-.10
Initial faculty selection--woman	.03	-.10	.23	.12
Tenure review--minority	.19	-.35	-.32	-.24
Tenure review--woman	.16	-.26	-.38	.10
Salary consideration--minority	.04	.19	-.04	-.04
Salary consideration--woman	-.06	-.21	-.21	-.19
Mentoring by senior colleagues--minority	-.16	-.22	-.42	.06
Mentoring by senior colleagues--woman	-.02	-.15	-.23	.44

Note: Respondents assessed the level of pressure that they felt about salary on the following scale:

No or Slight Pressure		Moderate Pressure		Excessive Pressure
1	2	3	4	5

In sum, only fourteen out of the thirty-two cross-tabulations result in noteworthy gammas, indicating that the relationship between the job satisfaction variable "feeling trapped in a profession with limited opportunity" and the perception of it being an advantage or disadvantage to be a minority or woman scholar with regard to important career dimensions, is not terribly strong. Once again, neither the strength nor the direction of the associations that do obtain are consistent across categorical groups on any of the career dimensions, indicating that important differences are likely to exist among the racial and categorical groups.

Table 6.7 reports gammas for the crosstabulations of the job satisfaction variable "feeling that my career progress is not what it should be" with the selected impact on career progress variables. Many of the gammas, for example, the black men's responses to mentoring by senior colleagues for minorities, are negative (gamma = -0.42), indicating an inverse relationship. That is, those feeling relatively high levels of pressure from the belief that their career progress is not what it should be also tend to feel that it is a disadvantage to be a minority with regard to mentoring by senior colleague; or, conversely, those who feel their career progress has been in line with their own expectations tend to feel that it is an advantage to be a minority with regard to mentoring by senior colleagues. All of the noteworthy gammas for the career progress variable, with the exception of black males' responses to initial faculty selection of women (gamma = 0.23) and black women's responses to the mentoring by senior colleagues for women (gamma = 0.44), indicate an inverse relationship. In the first case, the 0.23 gamma for black male responses to initial faculty selection for women indicates that as black males feel more pressure that their career progress is not what it should be, they tend to feel that it is an advantage to be a woman in regard to initial faculty selection. An examination of the cross-tabulation reveals that, indeed, 60.3 percent of the black males believe it is an advantage to be a woman in regard to initial faculty selection, with 14.7 percent and 25.0 percent of black males perceiving that it "makes no difference" or is a "disadvantage" to be a woman, respectively.

It should also be noted that for white males, none of the gamma statistics is noteworthy, indicating that the correlations between feeling pressure that one's career progress is not what it should be and attitudes about career progress and minority and women scholars are particularly weak for this group. Cross-tabulations of the job satisfaction variable "feeling that my career progress is not what it should be" and the selected impact on career dimensions for black males, however, result in noteworthy gammas on six of the eight career progress dimensions. Such gammas suggest that the correlation between the perception that one's own career progress is not what it should be and the career progress dimensions for impacts on minority and women scholars is uncharacteristically strong for this particular group of faculty.

The general distribution of the responses on the cross-tabulation tables is similar to that of the others, in that white males consistently express the belief that it is a disadvantage to be a woman or minority scholar in smaller proportions than any other race and gender sub-

Figure 6.3
Expression of Belief in Meritocracy

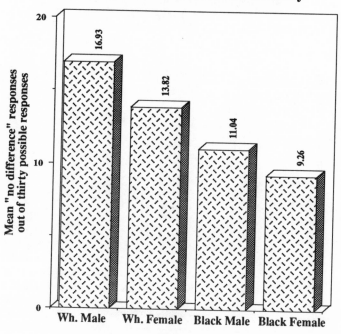

Faculty Groups

group. For example, only 6.1 percent of the white males perceived
that it was a disadvantage to be a minority with regard to tenure
review, while 23.2, 58.2 and 58.1 percent of white women, black
men and black women, respectively, believed minority status to be a
disadvantage with regard to tenure review. It follows from this that
in every case but one, greater percentages of white males also perceive that it is an advantage to be a woman or minority. In that one
exception, a higher percentage of black males believe that it is an
advantage to be a woman with regard to mentoring by senior colleagues than do the other groups (18.3 percent of black males versus
13.0 percent of white males, 7.8 percent of white females and 16.0
percent of black females). Similar to the gammas reported in Tables
6.4 and 6.5, there is no consistent pattern across the responses of the

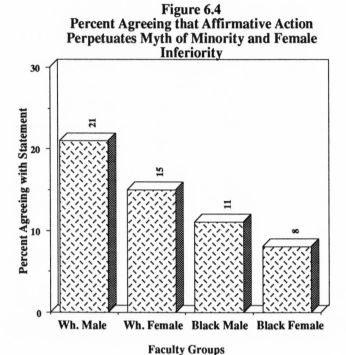

Figure 6.4
Percent Agreeing that Affirmative Action
Perpetuates Myth of Minority and Female
Inferiority

four categorical groups with regard to either the strength or the direction of the relationship between "feeling pressure that one's career progress is not what it should be" and the perception that it is an advantage or disadvantage to be a minority or woman scholar with regard to important career dimensions.

MEASURES OF CONFIDENCE IN MERITOCRACY

In Chapter 5 it was argued that the extent to which university faculty believe in the existence of meritocracy within academia could be assessed in part by examining the degree to which they felt that it made no difference to be a minority or woman scholar with regard to important career dimensions. Figure 6.3 displays the mean number of "no difference" responses given by each of the gender/ race categorical groups on the thirty career dimension variables. An examination of Figure 6.3 indicates that white males most frequently chose the "no difference" response (16.93 "no difference" responses out of 30). The number of times that "no difference" was

Figure 6.5
Percent Agreeing that Affirmative Action
Robs Groups of Accomplishment

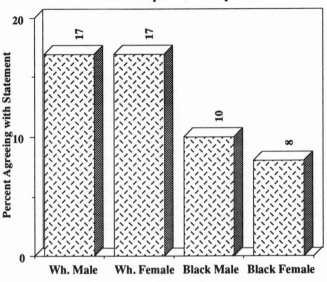

Faculty Groups

chosen by the respondents falls steadily moving from white males to white females to black males to black females. White women chose the "no difference" option an average of 13.82 times out of 30; black males chose "no difference" an average of 11.04 times out of 30; and black women chose "no difference" an average of 9.26 times out of 30. This same continuum was used to demonstrate the relative threat to one's self-interest from affirmative action in Figures 6.1 and 6.2. The trend for the expression of belief in meritocracy is the opposite of the trend for support of affirmative action, with belief in meritocracy being highest among the groups least likely to benefit from the implementation of affirmative action policies.

EXTENT OF AGREEMENT WITH CRITICISMS OF AFFIRMATIVE ACTION

In Chapter 5 it was argued that it was unclear to what extent respondents adhered to statements critical of affirmative action.

Figures 6.4 and 6.5 display the percentage of each racial/gender categorical group that expressed agreement with these two ideas: affirmative action perpetuates the myth of minority and female inferiority; and affirmative action robs women and minorities of a deserved sense of accomplishment. Figure 6.4 demonstrates clearly that the percentage of respondents agreeing with the statement that affirmative action perpetuates the myth of inferiority falls steadily as one moves along the continuum from white males to black females. Twenty-one percent of the white males agree with the statement, while 15 percent, 11 percent and 8 percent of white females, black males and black females, respectively, agree with the statement that affirmative action perpetuates the myth of minority and female inferiority. The same pattern holds in Figure 6.5, in which the percentage agreeing that affirmative action robs women and minorities of a sense of accomplishment falls as one moves from white males through the array of subgroups to black females. In this case, however, the same percentage of white males and white females agree with the statement (17 percent), while 10 percent of black males and 8 percent of black females agree that affirmative action robs minorities and women of a sense of accomplishment. These figures seem to indicate that self-interest is indeed a major factor in determining attitudes about affirmative action. Those most threatened by affirmative action express the most belief in the "myths" about affirmative action and show the least support for the policy both in the general and in the specific sense (see Figures 6.1 and 6.2).

The broader implications of these findings, and those reported earlier, are presented in the concluding chapter to follow. Along with a summary of empirical findings, some directions for further research in this important area of public policy are identified. Some speculations are offered on the fundamental question of the relative importance of self-interest and a "genuine concern to do the right thing" as motivations underlying the formulation of attitudes on public policy issues relating to social equity.

7

Conclusions

In Chapter 2 it was argued that affirmative action is a particularly interesting public policy to study within liberal societies because it gives rise to a conflict between the deeply held but sometimes incompatible values of individualism and egalitarianism. Affirmative action was described as "problematic" in American society because in order to achieve one "good"--that of a more equitable representation of women and minorities in the work force-- another "good"--the protection of the procedural safeguards of individual rights for white males--has to be compromised to some degree. The resolution of the conflict between these contending values was described on two levels: that of the character of value tradeoffs in the larger society, and that of the tension of competing values within individuals with respect to their feelings about policies intended to promote equality at the expense of the more advantaged individuals. The society's attempt to resolve this conflict of values was explained in the context of the statutory and judicial background to affirmative action. The decisions of the Supreme Court especially reflect the desire to protect both the procedural safeguards of equal protection and due process afforded to individuals and the policy goal of increasing the educational and employment opportunities of minorities and women in the work force. It was argued that university faculty provide a particularly interesting group in which to study the resolution of the micro level conflict in regard to attitudes about affirmative action inasmuch as academics have the somewhat unusual capability of making collegial hiring and promotional decisions. University faculty are also deeply enmeshed in a meritocratic system of professional peer review, anonymous evaluation of scholarship and so on.

The role of self-interest and its importance within liberal political systems was explored in Chapter 2. The legitimate pursuit of one's own self-interest was described as a "given" not only in the premises underlying liberal theory but also in the approach to understanding human behavior guiding much modern social science as well. How self-interest relates to the policy of affirmative action is one of the chief questions of this study. The resolution of the conflict mentioned above between the needs of protecting the individual versus the need to achieve some society-wide goal can be translated into a conflict between the self-interest of the individual and the needs of the larger collective. Affirmative action presents an interesting arena in which to study the resolution of such value conflicts because in some cases, namely that of white males, individuals face the possibility that their self-interest may be adversely affected in order to achieve the societal goal of enhancing the employment opportunity of women and minorities (Margolis 1982:6-16).

In an attempt to begin to understand the resolution of this conflict in Chapter 6, the respondents to the National Faculty Stress Study were arrayed along a continuum of posited self-interest based on their categorical group membership and the potential harm or benefit to their career to be experienced from the policy of affirmative action. The graphical representations of the respondents' attitudes toward affirmative action indicated that positive evaluations of the impacts of the policy both in regard to its general impacts on universities and on the respondents' own careers was highest among those most likely to benefit from the policy (black females), and was lowest among those most likely to be harmed from the policy (white males). When respondents' reactions to statements that affirmative action perpetuates the myth of female and minority inferiority and robs women and minorities of a sense of accomplishment were arrayed on the same continuum of self-interest, support for these statements was found to be highest among those most likely to be harmed by affirmative action (white males), and lowest among those most likely to benefit (black females). That is to say, the posited self-interest of the respondents based on their potential harm or benefit from affirmative action clearly distinguished the categorical groupings one from another in the expected direction. Self-interest based upon categorical group membership clearly differentiated the faculty respondents.

In Chapter 5 academia was described as a system of professional employment in which the ideal situation involves entrance into and career progress within a gradated status system based on meritocratic achievement. In this ideal system it was posited that individuals are judged by their peers according to their academic abilities--that is, their teaching, research and service accomplishments. In the ideal form of this system, race and gender would have no role. If categorical group membership were not an important correlate of professional attitudes or preferences, then academics should resemble one another without regard to racial and gender characteristics in their attitudes toward affirmative action.

In order to assess the extent to which racial/gender categorical group membership did distinguish faculty members and their attitudes, several analyses were conducted on the empirical evidence gathered in the National Faculty Stress Study. The results of these analyses indicated the extent to which the categorical groups differed (often in statistically significant ways) in their opinions about affirmative action and the impact of being a minority or female on career progress. A matched-pairs sample was used to control for intervening factors that might account for differences between white and black and between male and female faculty respondents such as type of academic discipline, tenure status, type of institution, marital status and age. In spite of the controls imposed by the matched-pairs sample, important and statistically significant differences were found between black and white faculty in the difference of means tests for matched pairs of university faculty. White respondents were inclined to argue that it was an advantage to be a minority with regard to career progress at higher rates than black faculty across all thirty career progress variables. Each of these means differed statistically at the 0.001 level, suggesting that the difference was indeed marked.

A second test of the extent to which the racial/gender categorical groups differed with regard to their attitudes about the impact of being a minority or woman scholar on career progress involved the use of a varimax-rotated factor analysis. The factor analysis was conducted separately for the black and white respondents on the questions that assessed the extent to which the respondents believed that it was an advantage, a disadvantage, or made no difference to be a minority or woman scholar with regard to important career dimensions. The discussion of findings set forth in Chapter 6 focused on several important differences in the way in which the factors loaded for white and black faculty emerged. The career progress variables on the highest loading factor for the two groups were distinctly different, with white respondents' highest loading factor consisting of concerns related to interpersonal communication, and black respondents' highest loading factor consisting of concerns related to pay and promotional opportunities. In addition, the factor analysis for black faculty respondents produced some variables that loaded on separate factors--such as mentoring by senior colleagues and initial faculty selection--that were included among other variables in the factor analysis for white respondents. Given that these two career progress variables are often cited as problematic for minority scholars to a greater extent than for white scholars, this result seems most reasonable. In sum, the factor analysis provided additional support for the conclusion that faculty respondents do indeed differ on the basis of categorical groupings in their attitudes about the impact of being a minority or woman scholar with regard to career progress.

In Chapter 5 it was suggested that other factors relevant to university faculty might also be associated with their attitudes about affirmative action; factors such as tenure status and job satisfaction constitute two examples of such factors. In order to assess the extent to which this line of reasoning might be true, cross-tabulations were conducted of the tenure status and job satisfaction variables with selected variables indicating the impact of minority or female status on career progress. Gamma statistics expressing the strength of the relationship between tenure status, three job satisfaction variables ("feeling pressure from receiving an inadequate salary to meet one's needs," "feeling trapped in a profession with limited opportunity" and "feeling pressure that my career progress is not what it should be") and the belief that it is an advantage, a disadvantage or makes no difference to be a minority or woman scholar with regard to career progress variables were reported in Chapter 6. The job satisfaction and tenure status variables were not consistently related to the respondents' perception of the impact of minority or female status on career progress across categorical groups in either the strength of the relationship or the direction in which that statistical relationship held. The fact that the pattern of the relationships across categorical groups is mixed, and that the strength and direction of the relationship between job satisfaction, tenure status and impact on career progress is different for the various categorical groups suggests that the impact of categorical group membership persists. The relatively small number of noteworthy gamma statistics for the relationship between the job satisfaction and tenure status variables and impact on career progress variables suggests that these factors are not associated in a meaningful way. These factors related to job satisfaction and professional life situation are thus weakly associated with attitudes about the impact of minority or female status on career progress.

In sum, the results of this analysis suggest that self-interest is indeed an important factor in determining attitudes about affirmative action. Racial and gender categorical group membership, which can be held to be associated with perceived self-interest with regard to affirmative action as well as in opposition to the presumption of a race and gender-neutral academy, distinguishes university faculty in their attitudes about affirmative action and the impact of minority or female status on career progress in statistically significant ways. Other factors, which might be held to be important in determining attitudes about this policy if categorical group membership were not an overriding factor in the shaping of such attitudes--such as job satisfaction and tenure status--are weakly associated with attitudes about the impact of minority or female status on career progress. The fact that the pattern of these relationships differs across categorical groups further suggests the importance of one's own categorical group membership to the formation of attitudes about affirmative action.

IMPLICATIONS OF FINDINGS

The history of affirmative action has been marked by serious opposition from many quarters. Challenges have come through litigation intended to block affirmative action plans or dispute their constitutionality, as well as from a presidential administration that openly opposed the concept of affirmative action and sought to defuse the administrative agencies responsible for its implementation and regulation (Steel and Lovrich 1987). Although affirmative action has become an entrenched part of the personnel function, it appears that the commitment to the spirit of affirmative action as originally conceived may be declining. In Chapter 1 the familiar story of the two shackled runners was offered as an explanation of the logic behind affirmative action. Noticing that one of the two runners is shackled halfway through the race, what shall we do now that the shackles have been removed? Shall we give the previously shackled runner a head start? While the analogy of the two runners offered in Chapter 1 at one time led decision-makers to conclude that the previously shackled runner ought to have a head start, it appears that decision-makers are more recently concerned with the effect on the previously unshackled runner that the head start allows. Recent Supreme Court rulings, for example, insist on a strict demonstration that the loss of benefits incurred by white males be justified by a pattern of previously existing discriminatory practices [see *City of Richmond v. Croson* US (1989)].

Affirmative action remains a problematic public policy in our society because it calls into question the appropriate balance between preserving the procedural safeguards afforded to white males and achieving increased racial and gender equity in the work force. Whether one chooses to discuss this policy in terms of "opening opportunities for historically disadvantaged groups" or exercising "preferential treatment," or terming it "correcting or compensating for past or present discrimination" or "reverse discrimination," the dilemma of achieving this balance between competing values remains. Deborah Stone contends that the "essence of policy making in political communities" is "the struggle over ideas" (1988:7). The way that a situation is defined is critical to the ultimate policy directives which will be undertaken. She explains that political reasoning is an attempt to try "to get others to see a situation as one thing or another" (Stone 1988:6). The proponents and opponents of affirmative action approach each other with different systems of language, focusing on conflicting "goods" at stake in this problematic policy area. Proponents of affirmative action focus on the "good" of increasing the racial and gender equity of our work force, and use language that addresses eliminating and compensating for historical barriers to minority and female entrance to the labor market. Opponents of affirmative action focus on the "good" of protecting procedural safeguards for individuals embodied in systems of merit, and use language that warns of reverse discrimination and preferential treatment. Each actor in the conflict tries to influence the perception of the problem and the primary value to be maintained, and hence predetermine what actions in behalf of protected class individuals are required and/or permissible as a result.

It is quite possible that the discrepancies in the perceptions of the various categorical groups in this study with regard to affirmative action reflect just such a divergence over the proper language and value to be emphasized. Perhaps it is such that white male academics as opposed to black and women academics choose as primary the preservation of procedural safeguards for individuals based on merit systems, while black and female academics choose as primary the increased number or women and minorities in academia. It remains consistent with self-interest for white males to articulate most clearly an opposition to affirmative action based on a high valuation of procedural safeguards for individuals that would disallow any form of preferential hiring. It is also consistent with self-interest for blacks and women to perceive affirmative action in a positive light, and emphasize the compensation for and elimination of historical discrimination.

The divergence in views across categorical groups relative to affirmative action discussed in this study points toward the potential for increased conflict over the implementation of affirmative action in the future. If the difference in attitudes about affirmative action and the relative advantage or disadvantage of women and minority scholars continues to be marked between white male academics and minority and female academics, the successful integration of greater numbers of women and minority scholars into the academy seems somewhat problematic. The collegial hiring and promotional decision structures used in American universities will only serve to highlight the different perceptions and languages that the various categorical groups bring to their understanding of affirmative action. It is perhaps this sort of fundamental disagreement over principles and core values that may make the acceptance of the few women and minority scholars currently in academia more difficult.

DIRECTIONS FOR FURTHER RESEARCH

Increased understanding of this topic suggests two primary directions that future research should continue or begin. In the first case, in order to understand the actual impact of affirmative action, or the need for such a policy, adequate tracking of the hiring and promotional decisions made by American universities must be continued. It is necessary to try to estimate the potential pool of minority and women scholars in order to know if, perhaps, a proportion of women and minority academics is being utilized that is equal to or greater than the number of adequately trained women and minority applicants. Or, conversely, this information will demonstrate the extent to which existing hiring and promotion decisions within an institution fall short of utilizing the proportion of adequately trained minority or women scholars.

A second direction that future research should focus on is the collection of more qualitative information regarding public perceptions of affirmative action. The use of survey research is fraught with the need for caveats concerning the generalizability and validity of the information obtained. Intensive interviewing to ascertain the extent to which various values and decision rules are employed by faculty involved in collegial hiring decisions would be a tremendous insight into the impact of values on the implementation of affirmative action in higher education. The extended insights of university faculty in all types of institutions nationally would allow an analysis more indepth than that possible in mail surveys.

In closing, perhaps Bellah et al. (1985) are correct in their assessment that Americans no longer have the language of public concern that de Tocqueville found in the 1800s. The finding that racial and gender categorical group membership is the overriding determinant of attitudes about affirmative action suggests that while Kelman's analysis of a "hopeful" view of U.S. government is attractive, it would appear to be more akin to wishful thinking than a true reflection of human behavior in politics.

Bibliography

Arthur, John, and William H. Shaw. (1978). *Justice and Economic Distribution*. Englewood Cliffs, NJ: Prentice-Hall.

Barber, Benjamin R. (1979). "The Compromised Republic: Public Purposelessness in America," in Robert H. Horwitz (ed.), *The Moral Foundations of the American Republic*, 2nd edn, pp. 19-38. Charlottesville: University of Virginia Press.

Bellah, Robert N. (1980). *Varieties of Civil Religion*. San Francisco: Harper and Row.

Bellah, Robert N., Richard Madsen, William M. Sullivan, Ann Swidler and Steven M. Tipton. (1985). *Habits of the Heart: Individualism and Commitment in American Life*. New York: Harper and Row.

Bigland, Arthur. (1973). "The Characteristics of Subject Matter in Academic Areas," *Journal of Applied Psychology*. 57 (June):195-203.

Blalock, Hubert M., Jr. (1979). *Social Statistics*, 2nd edn. New York: McGraw Hill.

Bowen, Howard, and Jack Schuster. (1986). *American Professors: A National Resource Imperiled*. New York: Oxford University Press.

Brown, Shirley Vining. (1988). *Increasing Minority Faculty: An Elusive Goal*. A research report of the Minority Graduate Education Project, jointly sponsored by the Graduate Record Examinations Board and Educational Testing Service.

Buchanan, James M., and Gordon Tullock. (1962). *The Calculus of Consent*. Ann Arbor: University of Michigan Press.

Bulletin/Calendar for Faculty and Staff of Washington State University. (1979). "Affirmative Action Policy Presented for Review." Vol. 5, May 25, 1979, p. 3.

Carens, Joseph H. (1981). *Equality, Moral Incentives, and the Market: An Essay in Utopian Politics-Economic Theory.* Chicago: University of Chicago Press.

Carnegie Foundation for the Advancement of Teaching (CHE). (1985). "Carnegie Foundation Survey of Faculty Members," *The Chronicle of Higher Education.* (December 18).

City of Richmond v. J.A. Croson [U.S. (1989)].

Cohen, Marshall, Thomas Nagel and Thomas Scanlon (eds). (1988). *Equality and Preferential Treatment.* Princeton, NJ: Princeton University Press.

Cole, Jonathan R. (1979). *Fair Science: Women in the Scientific Community.* New York: The Free Press.

Dahl, Robert A. (1977). "On Removing Certain Impediments to Democracy in the United States," *Political Science Quarterly.* 92:1-20.

Daniels, Lee A. (1989). "Ranks of Black Men Shrink on U.S. Campuses." *New York Times*, Sunday, February 5, p.1.

DeFunis v. Odegaard and the University of Washington [416 U.S. 312 (1974)].

Dillman, Donald A. (1978). *Mail and Telephone Surveys: The Total Design Method.* New York: Wiley.

Downs, Anthony. (1957). *An Economic Theory of Democracy.* New York: Harper and Row.

Dworkin, Ronald. (1977). *Taking Rights Seriously.* Cambridge: Harvard University Press.

Fiorina, Morriss. (1977). *Congress: Keystone of the Washington Establishment.* New Haven: Yale University Press.

Fox, Mary Frank. (1984). "Women and Higher Education: Sex Differentials in the Status of Students and Scholars." in Jo Freeman (ed.), *Women: a Feminist Perspective*, pp.238-55. Palo Alto: Mayfield.

Frank, Anne H., and Jacqueline W. Mintz. (1987). "Four Trends in Higher Education Law," *Academe* (September-October):57-63.

Frederickson, H. George. (1980). *New Public Administration.* Tuscaloosa: University of Alabama Press.

Fullilove et al. v. Klutznick [448 U.S. 448 (1980)].

Gallup, George Jr. (1984). *The Gallup Poll.* Wilmington, DE: Scholarly Resources, Inc.

_____ (1987). *The Gallup Poll.* Wilmington, DE: Scholarly Resources, Inc.

Garcia, Luis, Nancy Erskine, Kathy Hawn and Susanne R. Casmay. (1981). "The Effect of Affirmative Action on Attributions About Minority Group Members," *Journal of Personality* 49:427-37.

Gill, Gerald R. (1980). *Meanness Mania The Changed Mood.* Washington, DC: Howard University Press.

Glazer, Nathan. (1975). *Affirmative Action: Ethnic Inequality and Public Policy.* New York: Basic Books.

Gmelch, Walter, Nicholas P. Lovrich and P. Kay Wilke. (1984). "Stress in Academe: A National Perspective," *Research in Higher Education.* 20:447-90.

Gmelch, Walter, Phyllis Kay Wilke and Nicholas P. Lovrich. (1986). "Dimensions of Stress Among University Faculty: Factor Analytic Results from a National Study." *Research in Higher Education.* 24:266-86.

Griggs v. Duke Power Company [401 U.S. 424 (1971)].

Hankin, Joseph N. (1985). "Where the (Affirmative) Action is (or is not): the Status of Minorities and Women Among the Faculty and Administrators of Public Two-Year Colleges, 1983-1984." Mimeograph. Valhalla, NY: Westchester Community College.

Hawkins, Brett W., Mary Ann E. Steger and Jean Trimble. (1986). "How (Some) Community Organizations Adapt to Fiscal Strain," *Research in Urban Policy.* 2:117-25.

Hays, William. (1973). *Statistics for the Social Sciences.* New York: Holt Rhinehart.

Heidenheimer, Arnold J., Hugh Heclo and Carolyn Teich Adams. (1975). *Comparative Public Policy: The Politics of Social Choice in Europe and America.* New York: St. Martin's Press.

Horwitz, Robert H. (1979). "John Locke and the Preservation of Liberty: A Perennial Problem of Civic Education," in Robert Horwitz (ed.), *The Moral Foundations of the American Republic*, 2nd edn, pp.129-56. Charlottesville: University of Virginia Press.

Inglehart, Ronald, and Jacques-Rene Rabier. (1986). "Political Realignment in Advanced Industrial Society: From Class-Based Politics to Quality of Life Politics," *Government and Opposition* 21:456-79.

Johnson v. Transportation Agency, Santa Clara County, California [107 S. Ct. 1442 (1987)].

Kariel, Henry S. (1977). *Beyond Liberalism, Where Relations Grow.* San Francisco: Chandler and Sharp.

Kelman, Steven. (1987). "Public Choice and Public Spirit," *The Public Interest.* 87 (Spring):80-94.

Kinder, Donald R. and D. Roderick Kieweit. (1979). "Economic Discontent and Political Behavior: The Role of Personal Grievances and Collective Economic Judgements in Congressional Voting," *American Journal of Political Science.* 23:495-529.

Lasch, Christopher. (1979). *The Culture of Narcissism: American Life in An Age of Diminishing Expectations.* New York: W.W. Norton and Co.

Lipset, Martin Seymour and William Schneider. (1978). "The Bakke Case: How Would it be Decided at the Bar of Public Opinion?" *Public Opinion* 1:38-44.

Madison, James. *Federalist #51*, reprinted in Susan Welch, John Gruhl, Michael Steinman and John Comer (1988) *American Government* 2nd edn. New York: West Publishing Co.

Margolis, Howard. (1982). *Selfishness, Altruism, Rationality: A Theory of Social Choice.* Chicago: University of Chicago Press.

Martin et al. v. Wilks [U.S. (1989)]

Mayhew, David. (1974). *Congress: The Electoral Connection.* New Haven: Yale University Press.

McCormack, Wayne (ed.). (1978). *The Bakke Decision: Implications for Higher Education Admissions.* A report of the American Council on Education-Association of American Law Schools Committee on Bakke. Washington, DC: ACE-AALS.

McWilliams, Wilson Carey. (1979). "On Equality as the Moral Foundation for Community," in Robert H. Horwitz (ed.), *The Moral Foundations of the American Republic*, 2nd edn, pp. 183-213. Charlottesville: University of Virginia Press.

Mooney, Christopher F., S.J. (1982). *Inequality and the American Conscience: Justice Through The Judicial System.* New York: Paulist Press.

Nacoste, Rupert W. (1985). "Selection Procedures and Responses to Affirmative Action the Case of Favorable Treatment," *Law and Human Behavior.* 9:225-42.

Nagel, Rhea A. (1988). "Minorities in Higher Education," *Journal of Career Planning and Employment* 48:45-46.

Nagel, Thomas. (1977). "Equal Treatment and Compensatory Discrimination," in Marshall Cohen, Thomas Nagel and Thomas Scanlon (eds), *Equality and Preferential Treatment*, pp. 3-18. Princeton, NJ: Princeton University Press.

Nalbandian, John. (1989). "The U.S. Supreme Court's 'Consensus' on Affirmative Action," *Public Administration Review* 47:38-45.

Okun, Arthur M. (1975). *Equality and Efficiency: The Big Tradeoff.* Washington, DC: The Brookings Institute.

Orren, Gary R. (1988). "Beyond Self Interest," in Robert B. Reich (ed.), *The Power of Public Ideas*, pp.13-29. Cambridge, MA: Ballinger.

Pitre, Merline. (1981). "Scholar's Reactions to Bakke," *The Western Journal of Black Studies* 5:82-6.

Rasnic, Carol D. (1988). "The Supreme Court and Affirmative Action: An Evolving Standard or Compounded Confusion?" *Employee Relations Law Journal* 14:175-90.

Rawls, John. (1978). "'A Theory of Justice' and 'The Basic Structure as Subject'" in John Arthur and William H. Shaw (eds), *Justice and Economic Distribution*, pp.18-52. Englewood Cliffs, NJ: Prentice Hall.

Reed, Rodney. (1985). "Faculty Diversity: An Educational and Moral Imperative in Search of Institutional Commitment," in *Vital Issues: The Future of Affirmative Action and Desegregation in Higher Education.* Proceedings from the Clemson University Regional Conference, September 17-20, 1985, Clemson, South Carolina, pp. 22-39.

Regents of the University of California v. Bakke [438 U.S. 265 (1978)].

Rice, Mitchell F., and Woodrow Jones, Jr. (1984). "Introduction: Public Policy and Black Americans," in Mitchell F. Rice and Woodrow Jones, Jr. (eds), *Contemporary Public Policy Perspectives and Black Americans: Issues in an Era of Retrenchment Politics*, pp. 3-13. Westport, CT: Greenwood Press.

Rohr, John A. (1987). "The Administrative State and Constitutional Principle," in Ralph Chandler (ed.), *A Centennial History of the American Administrative State*, pp. 113-161. New York: The Free Press.

Rossum, Ralph A. (1980). *Reverse Discrimination: the Constitutional Debate.* New York: Marcel Dekker.

Sandel, Michael. (1982). *Liberalism and the Limits of Justice.* Cambridge: Cambridge University Press.

Seligman, Daniel. (1973). "How 'Equal Opportunity' Turned in to Quotas," *Fortune* 87:160-68.

Seltzer, Richard, and Edward Thompson. (1985). *Attitudes Towards Discrimination and Affirmative Action For Minorities and Women.* Mimeograph. Institute for Urban Affairs and Research, Howard University, Washington, DC (February).

Sindler, Allan P. (1978). *Bakke, DeFunis, and Minority Admissions: The Quest for Equal Opportunity.* New York: Longman.

Sisneros, Anthony Adolph. (1984). *Receptivity to Affirmative Action in Higher Education: A Study of Minority, White Male and Administrative Attitudes Toward Minority Preference.* Ph.D. dissertation, Washington State University.

Skidmore, Max J. (1978). *American Political Thought.* New York: St. Martin's Press.

Smith, Earl, and Stephanie L. Witt. (forthcoming). "Faculty Attitudes Toward Affirmative Action: The Academic Ethos in Question," *The Western Journal of Black Studies.*

Sniderman, Paul, and Michael Gray Hagen. (1985). *Race and Inequality A Study of American Values.* Chatham, NJ: Chatham House.

Sowell, Thomas. (1975). *Affirmative Action Reconsidered: Was it Necessary in Academia?* Washington DC: American Enterprise Institute for Public Policy Research.

Steel, Brent S., and Nicholas P. Lovrich. (1987). "Equality and Efficiency Tradeoffs in Affirmative Action--Real or Imagined? The Case of Women in Policing," *The Social Science Journal.* 24:53-70.

Stone, Deborah. (1988). *Policy Paradox and Political Reason.* Glenview, IL: Scott Foresman.

Stout, Jeffrey. (1986). "Liberal Society and the Language of Morals," *Soundings.* 69:32-59.

U.S. Civil Rights Commission. (1979). *Understanding Bakke.* Washington DC: U.S. Civil Rights Commission.

U.S. Steelworkers of America v. Weber [443 U.S. 193 (1979)].

Waldo, William S., and Bernadette M. Davison. (1987). "Renewed Affirmative Action Enforcement is Emminent," *Personnel Journal.* 66:55-75.

Wards Cove Packing Co. Inc. et al. v. Atonio et al. [U.S. (1989)].

Washington State University (WSU) Affirmative Action Office.(1987). Information About Affirmative Action.

Wilke, Phyllis Kay, Walter Gmelch and Nicholas Lovrich. (1985)."Stress and Productivity: Evidence of the Inverted U Function in a National Study of University Faculty," *Public Productivity Review.* 12:342-356.

Witt, Stephanie L., and Nicholas P. Lovrich. (1988). "Sources of Stress Among Faculty: Gender Differences." *The Review of Higher Education.* 11:269-83.

Wolin, Sheldon. (1960). *Politics and Vision.* Boston: Little, Brown and Company.

Woodard, Michael D. (1982). "Ideological Response to Alterations in the Structure of Oppression: Reverse Discrimination, the Current Racial Ideology in the U.S.," *The Western Journal of Black Studies* 6:166-74.

Wygant et al. v. Jackson Board of Education [106 S. Ct. 1842 1986)] .

Young, Michael. (1958). *The Rise of the Meritocracy, 1870-2033: An Essay on Education and Equality.* London: Thames and Hudson.

Index

About the Author

STEPHANIE L. WITT received her Ph.D. in Political Science from Washington State University. In addition to affirmative action, her research interests include issues in state and local government and urban service delivery. Her articles have appeared in the *Western Political Quarterly, Western Governmental Researcher, Western Journal of Black Studies* and the *Review of Higher Education.* She is currently an Assistant Professor of Political Science and Public Affairs at Boise State University.